Dining
with the
Dollar Diva

Divalicious Menus with Ingredients
Costing $1 or Less

Elizabeth J. Fisher

Dining with the Dollar Diva:
Divalicious Menus with Ingredients Costing $1 or Less

Published by
The Elevator Group
Paoli, Pennsylvania

Library of Congress Control Number: 2010923207

Trade Paperback: ISBN-10: 0982528248
              ISBN-13: 978-0-9825282-4-2

Jacket and interior design by Stephanie Vance-Patience

Published in the United States by The Elevator Group.

Photos by Elizabeth J. Fisher

This book was printed in the United States.

To order additional copies of this book, contact:
The Elevator Group
PO Box 207
Paoli, PA 19301
www.TheElevatorGroup.com
610-296-4966 (p) • 610-644-4436 (f)
info@TheElevatorGroup.com

Dedication

"I Can Do All Things Through Christ Who Strengthens Me"
—Philippians 4:13

I am truly grateful to my Lord and Savior Jesus Christ because with HIM I can do everything but fail. I thank God for giving me the courage to step out on faith and commit to the successful completion of this cookbook. This journey has been recipe of love; my love of Jesus, my love of family, love of my faithful supporters, my church and the congregation and a love of food!

I dedicate this book to my father, the late Nathaniel "Donald" Fisher, Sr. Daddy was the first person I remember who unashamedly purchased the "red, white and black" boxes from the old A&P grocery store before generics were in vogue. Daddy's phenomenal Sunday dinners that he cooked in the kitchen at 257 Kentucky Avenue are memorable to me. Daddy baked chicken that tasted like pheasant under glass. He doctored up Franco American macaroni and cheese in the yellow can so that we thought it was a family recipe passed down from generation to generation. He served us canned peas that looked like they were just picked from the garden that morning. And who could forget those Ann Page Parker House rolls that he would generously butter the tops of and reheat so anyone would think he spent the entire morning baking homemade rolls. No matter what I thought I wanted to do in my life, he supported me. My father was my biggest champion. I pray that Daddy is proud of me and would enjoy this cookbook.

Divalicious Menus with Ingredients Costing $1 or Less

Acknowledgments

Every day that I wake up is a blessed reminder that God is giving me the opportunity to live, not merely exist. In order to live you must love, trust, share, demonstrate compassion, breathe clean air and eat good food.

Some folk eat to live; I live to eat and cook.

I wish to thank……

▶ My son, Marques, who is the best part of me, and was my original taste tester. He constantly encouraged and motivated me by telling me, "Mom you can do this. There's a cookbook in the future for you. You just gotta do it!" He gave me the digital camera I use to take pictures for this cookbook.

▶ My mother, Lillian Battle, who has defeated every illness, hospitalization, chronic condition and nursing home that was thrown her way. Her perpetual determination and strong will was an excellent paradigm of inspiration that let me know that I'm cut from the same strong "Colen family" cloth! And that I too can succeed in anything that I put my mind to.

▶ My grandmother, Cepha Thornton, who taught me to love the Lord and chastised me that putting ketchup on my scrambled eggs is an insult to the person who cooked them.

▶ The matriarch and patriarch of our family, Aunt Ev and Uncle Ed, whose wisdom and loving compassion I know is always present.

▶ My stepson, Harold II, who I love dearly and who let me make hash with his filet mignon.

▶ My oldest sister, Bubbie, my protectress, who is always there to encourage and love me and allows me my "off the wall moments".

▶ My older sister Brenda, the best friend any sister could have! She will suit up and defend me in a heartbeat, anytime and anywhere, even if I'm dead wrong.

- My brothers, Donnie and Tommy, who were more enthusiastic about this project than I expected.
- My brother-in-law, Rev. Dr. Uncle Sonny Berry, who will always tell me that I bake the sweetest sweets.
- Debbie Harley, my neighbor, who was always there for walks, talks, vents, texts and serious gossip sessions, "gossip....ooooppps, did I say that out loud?"
- My Aunti Barbara, who instilled in me the joy of cooking, gracious entertaining, and knowing good food.
- My Pastor, Rev. Carlos D. Bounds, who prays for me and consistently tells me that I am destined to begin a new and better life filled with joy, happiness, and success!
- My Associate Pastor, Rev. Mary Ellen Collier, who is there to listen and teaches me to pray unceasingly.
- Uncle Luigi and Ms. Peg, for your support and wonderful friendship.
- The members of the Bethel AME Church, Bryn Mawr, Tuesday afternoon Bible Study class who were surreptitiously chosen to be my taste testers.
- Ms. Patsy, for her perpetual support and excellent feedback.
- Ms. Francis who, unknowingly, had agreed to be my proofreader.
- I would be remiss if I didn't mention my stepfather John "Jackie" Battle who loved me unconditionally, even when I gave him grief for all of those 10:30PM delicious Thanksgiving dinners he served, because he was slow as molasses in the kitchen.
- My publisher, Sheilah Vance, who didn't dismiss, blow me off or belittle me when I told her I wanted to write a cookbook — she encouraged me to write two!

I know that I have been truly and wondrously blessed because of all of you who helped me along the way with this delightfully satisfying and delicious endeavor.

Bless the hands that prepared the food!

Prologue...

Being the 5th of five children, I always got hand me downs — clothes, toys, books, etc. So, I'm used to getting "things" at a minimal price or no cost.

I remember shopping at the Merit Store in Ardmore, PA and getting bargains, but when I was advised that this chain was moving forward with the everything for a dollar concept, I was incensed, because I could only imagine the cheap, low quality trinkets that would be sold. But, being one never to turn her nose up at a bargain, I finally relented and visited the newly opened Dollar Express.

Oh, please, I was on cloud nine. There were aisles and aisles of good buys, and, yeah, I was that person on the commercial, asking, "How much?", and the cashier would roll her eyes in the back of her head and would give me the patent response, "Price check in aisle one." Then when the different dollar stores started selling foods and refrigerated items, I was in dollar store heaven.

Now, I could say that I had to watch my pennies being a single parent, raising my son on a tight budget, but truthfully, this Sista Girl likes to buy in bulk. So instead of purchasing one bottle of a brand name juice, or cleaning supplies, greeting cards, snacks, frozen and refrigerated items, et.al., at the local grocery stores, pharmacies, I could buy these exact items for $1. Ain't life grand!!

Dining With the Dollar Diva

Explanation...

The original premise of my cookbook was to provide delicious affordable meals where all of the ingredients were purchased from the $1 Stores. Over the years, many dollar stores had closed their doors forever, which is unfortunate, considering this economy. So shopping at the same $1 Stores was still cost-effective, but the menu diversity became stagnant.

However, big chain grocery stores jumped on the $1 bandwagon, and now you'll see their weekly supplements will advertise "10 for $10" sales. So, now I'm able to include even fresh meats, like chicken, at 10 lbs. for $10. Do the math. It's a $1/lb! You can even purchase ground turkey, smoked sausage, frozen 4 ounce bags of scallops, shrimp, and various fish filets at 10 for $10.

Being the brunt of many a "cheapskate" joke for getting the most for my $$$$, I've been known to shop at small, "eclectic", discount food stores, big box and stores that purchase overstock or discontinued items (that are still within date), where food items can be purchased for a $1 or less.

So, my cookbook transitioned to one where each ingredient cost $1 or less. (Even as I'm getting this book from solely $1 store purchases to print, my local grocery store is selling box pie crust 2/$1.) When I would come home from my shopping expeditions, my whole porch would be loaded down with tons of bags. I may have only spent a "couple of dollars", but I was truly satisfied because I knew I saved hundreds of dollars with the potential of thousands of meals I would be able to prepare.

Foreword...

Eating and cooking is a life long story for me, so I pray you find my recipe anecdotes to be interesting and humorous. But, I also hope that you'll enjoy my cost-cutting recipes where all ingredients are $1 or less to be exciting, delicious and easy to prepare. Just want to let you know that from time to time I will mention my son Marques, my Aunt Barbara, The Sterling Club, and my church family, Bethel AME Bryn Mawr, so you may want to get to know them on a first name basi right now. Cooking is an interactive sport, so don't hesitate to cook with your senses, sight, taste, touch and smell.

So... let's go food shopping, "How much is this?" "For you, $1".

Table of Contents

Main Course Entrées **59**

Divalicious Menus with Ingredients Costing $1 or Less

Divalicious Menus with Ingredients Costing $1 or Less

Divalicious Menus with Ingredients Costing $1 or Less

Hors d'oeuvres, Cocktail Snacks, & Appetizers

Hors d'oeuvres, Cocktail Snacks, & Appetizers

$1Diva Tips

$ All $1 Stores often have the identical basic inventory. But don't limit yourself to shopping at one $1 Store. Stores may stock different items.

$ Don't forget local supermarkets' 10-for-$10 sales. Always review your local supermarket and big box store weekly ads for great bargains.

$ Shopping at small ethnic stores is a great way to find low cost spices, herbs seasonings, extracts, and those special unique ingredients for $1 or less.

$ Check out your local produce stands. You can get outstanding $1 bargains for fresh fruit, vegetables, herbs, dried fruits and veggies, and spices. During the summer, you may also be able to get small potted herb plants for $1. Start your own pot garden and grow your own herbs.

$ You can find dried herbs, spices, and seasonings at the $1 Store and local drugstores for less than $1.

$ If a recipe calls for pie crust, you may be able to substitute with refrigerated biscuit dough, or pizza crust, and vice versa.

$ You'd be surprised what food items you can freeze. Go ahead and stock up. Just make sure you have room in your freezer.

$1Diva Legend

▶ S&P2T ....Salt and Pepper to Taste

▶ $1 ....Item purchased at $1 Store

▶ 10-4-$10 ....10 items for $10

▶ <$1 or no symbol................................ Item is less than $1

▶ $1/Fresh ....Purchase at $1 Store or use fresh

▶ S2YT...Season to Your Taste

▶ Pantry ....Item should be on hand in your pantry

Some items in these recipes will require flour, eggs, bread-crumbs, shortenings (butter/margarine; vegetable, corn and/or olive oils). You should have these items readily available in your pantry. If not, you may have to do a basic shopping expedition.

Muenster Cheese With Marmalade in Puffed Pastry

My Aunti Barbara always makes a baked brie in a puffed pastry appetizer for *The Sterling Club* Christmas parties. It is always a big hit. This is a modified version of that appetizer.

INGREDIENTS
8 oz block Muenster Cheese-cut in 1" cubes
(or any soft cheese) ....10-4-$10
1 pie crust ....$1 or <$1
4 oz orange marmalade
(or fruit preserves/jam of your choice) $1

DIRECTIONS
▶ Preheat oven to 425 degrees

▶ Prepare pizza crust according to package directions

▶ Place cheese cubes in center of pie crust

▶ Top cheese with the fruit jam/preserves

▶ Fold pie crust edges over one another so the cheese is covered

▶ Bake for approximately 20 minutes when crust is browned and cheese is softened/melted

▶ Serve with crackers and/or sliced apples or pears

$1Diva FYI

$ I know, I know, Muenster cheese, $1????!!!!! My local grocery store always has weekly 10 for $10 sales, and they have not only the 8 oz. chunk cheeses but the 8 oz. bags of shredded cheeses as well. I stocked up on a whole lot of cheese (cheddar, mozzarella, Muenster, Monterey Jack, Langhorne, Swiss), and I was able to get rainchecks for some of the cheeses that had sold out. Remember, always check your local grocery stores for their weekly $1 specials. That was how I was able to get the pizza crusts. If pie crust is not available, then just substitute with refrigerated biscuits. I strongly suggest that you use the flakey biscuits and roll them out to a 1/4 inch pastry crust.

Pineapple Salami Rollups

INGREDIENTS

1 package sliced Genoa salami/pepperoni
(use the large pepperoni slices) $1

8 oz cream cheese softened..<$1

4 pepperoncini peppers diced $1

8 oz canned pineapple tidbits-drained $1

2 tbsp minced garlic..$1

¼ cup parsley $1/Fresh

10 green onions

DIRECTIONS

▶ Lay out entire package of sliced salami on your cooking surface

▶ Wash and dry green onions

▶ Mix cream cheese with hand mixer, then fold in remaining ingredients, S&P2T

▶ Spread cream cheese mixture on each slice of salami and roll around green onion, seam side down

▶ Secure with toothpick and cover and refrigerate until you are ready to serve

$1Diva FYI

$ You can also use pepperoni for this quick and easy snack.

Breadsticks w/Marinara Sauce

It never fails that when my son, Marques, comes home for a visit and attends church with me, he never gets an opportunity to eat during the repast following the worship service. I guess because "HIS" proud mother is ordering him to speak to all of the members of the congregation. So by time he's finished, if you know Bethel like I know Bethel, the food is GONE!!!! Inevitably, Marques comes home hungry. Well, time after time of attending church worship and missing the repasts, I suggested to Marques to fix a plate. Especially this Sunday, because I had coordinated the baptism luncheon that included my baked ziti, which I know he loves. Marques may have fixed himself a plate to go, but being the absent-minded fella that he is, he forgot where he put his plate. So with his plate being MIA and the congregation having licked the pans of baked ziti clean, my poor baby went home starved. As soon as I got home, I took inventory of the remaining items that I brought home. I noticed that there was a bag of garlic bread sticks that hadn't been touched. Hmmmmmmm...... I was able to come up with this gratifying Italian fast-food snack.

INGREDIENTS

¾ c mozzarella cheese ....10-4-$10

1 package garlic breadsticks ....Pantry or $1

1 c marina sauce ....Pantry or $1

2 tbsp minced/chopped garlic ....Pantry or $1

¼ tsp sugar ....Pantry or $1

Sprinkle basil, oregano, SP2T.............................Pantry or $1

DIRECTIONS

▶ Preheat oven according to directions on breadsticks package

▶ Put breadsticks on baking sheet

▶ Top with mozzarella cheese

▶ Heat breadsticks in oven until thoroughly warmed and cheese melts. Then remove from oven and sprinkle with oregano and/or basil

▶ Microwave marinara sauce until warm, season with various Italian herbs

▶ Stir sugar and garlic into marina sauce

▶ To serve, pour marina sauce in bowl and dip breadsticks

Meatballs & Tuna Bites with Dipping Sauce

INGREDIENTS-Meatballs

8-oz bag turkey/beef meatballs -slightly thawed ......Pantry or $1

1 egg ....Pantry or $1

¼ cup water or milk ....Pantry or $1

½ cup bread crumbs ....Pantry or $1

1 c oil ....Pantry or $1

DIRECTIONS-Meatballs

▶ Beat egg and water/milk together. Dredge meatballs in egg and then bread crumbs. Let sit for a minute

▶ Place meatballs in saucepan when oil is hot (cooked meatballs will rise to top of oil)

▶ Remove from oil and S&P2T immediately while draining

▶ Skewer with toothpicks for dipping in sauce (sauces at end of this section)

INGREDIENTS-Tuna Bites

5-oz can tuna $1

2 tbsp cup minced onion ....Pantry or $1

3 tbsp mayonnaise...Pantry or $1

1 egg ....Pantry or $1

¼ cup water or milk...Pantry or $1

¼ cup bread crumbs $1

1 c oil ....Pantry or $1

DIRECTIONS: Tuna Bites

▶ Drain and flake tuna in small mixing bowl

▶ Mix onion, garlic powder, parsley and the 2 Tbsp breadcrumbs into the flaked tuna

▶ Shape into small bite size balls

▶ Beat egg and water/milk together

▶ Dredge tuna bites into the remaining breadcrumbs

▶ Place tuna bites in refrigerator for approximately 15 minutes to set

▶ Preheat oil on medium heat in a deep sauce pan

▶ Carefully place tuna bites into the heated oil

▶ Fry until brown

▶ Remove from oil and S&P2T immediately while draining

▶ Skewer with toothpicks for dipping in sauce (dipping sauces available at the end of this section)

Chicken Medallions w/Spicy Blue Cheese Dipping Sauce

INGREDIENTS

1 lb chicken breast ....10-4-$10

1/2 c flour ....Pantry or $1

1/2 c breadcrumbs ....Pantry or $1

1 tbsp thyme $1

1/2 oil ....Pantry or $1

S&P2T ....Pantry

DIRECTIONS

▶ Preheat oil in skillet

▶ Rinse and cut chicken breast at an angle into 1" thick medallions

▶ Mix flour and breadcrumbs together with thyme

▶ Dredge medallions into the flour mixture

▶ Place medallions into hot oil. Let fry until brown and crispy

▶ Drain and SP2T immediately after removing from oil

▶ Place on platter, skewer with toothpicks and serve with favorite dipping sauce

Pepperoni & Swiss Knots

This is a recipe that I must thank God for. I was working on my Ravioli Carbonara for test tasting, but I needed an accompanying side dish. All I had available was a can of refrigerated biscuits and pepperoni. I just couldn't do another garlic cheese bread thing. I started thinking about the time Victoria Hill, my church member and a former recruiting co-worker, and I went to the local Kmart for lunch. Before going back to the dreaded hell hole, I mean office, she stopped at her favorite deli for a hoagie. She said that she just had a taste for a pepperoni & Swiss cheese hoagie. Vicki said that she knew that it was a strange combination, but she just loved the blend of Swiss cheese and pepperoni. Being that I don't eat pork I couldn't ask for a taste, but it sounded absolutely delicious to me. Then God blessed me to put my culinary spin on these 3 ingredients. I had to keep reminding myself that every $1 or less ingredient does NOT have to come from the $1 Store. So guess what? I remembered that the grocery store had a 10 for $10 sale on their 8 oz chunk Swiss cheese. To help this Diva out, the sale included all of the 8oz chunk

cheeses and bags of shredded cheese, too. So you know I raced down to the neighborhood grocery store, and I stocked up on various cheeses like a bear preparing for its winter hibernation. When I returned home, I made this great appetizer, and they were absolutely beautiful. By the way, this small gastronomic tidbit is multi-dimensional. If you make small ones, they are a great cocktail snack. Make them larger, serve with a marinara sauce, and you can make them a meal. Be creative and use different fillings, like spinach & feta cheese, broccoli & cheddar. BTW, $1 Store NOW sells feta cheese!!!!!!

13

INGREDIENTS

1-8 oz package pepperoni $1

1/2 cup shredded swiss cheese ....10-4-$10

Sprinkle red pepper flakes $1

1/4 cup chopped garlic $1

Sprinkle basil, oregano, or Italian seasoning $1/fresh

1 roll refrigerated biscuit dough
   (I prefer using the flakey) ....10-4-$10 or <$1

1/2 stick butter/margarine ....<$1

Flour & cornmeal to dust surface to roll dough

DIRECTIONS

▶ Preheat oven to 325 degrees

▶ Dust baking sheet with flour & cornmeal

▶ Flour wax paper to roll out biscuits

▶ Separate the biscuits up to 2xs the amount listed on the package and roll the dough out to round disks slightly larger than the pepperoni

▶ Top with 1 slice of pepperoni and sprinkle with swiss cheese and garlic

▶ Roll into a log, and then fold in half and twist one half over the other. Twist both ends under the roll, and place on baking sheet

▶ Repeat until all of the knots are done

▶ Lightly brush each knot with butter/margerine

▶ Place in oven approximately 25 minutes or until brown

▶ Remove when knots are finished baking

▶ Lightly brush each knot with remaining butter

▶ Sprinkle with either basil, oregano, or Italian seasoning of your choice

$1Diva FYI

$ Dip knots in marinara sauce sprinkled with cheese, if desired.

Divalicious Menus with Ingredients Costing $1 or Less

Empanadas

Mucho años ago, when I attended Swedeland Elementary School I had a Spanish teacher named Mrs. Towes (pronounce toes), who came to my 2nd grade classroom every Tuesday and Thursday. Now keep in mind this was approximately 45 years ago, so I may have the days wrong, but she did come twice a week, and her name was Mrs. Towes. She was a wonderful woman. She always entered our classroom with a brilliant smile, and then she would start speaking Spanish with an accent that you would swear she was originally from Spain. With the help of my fifth grade brother Tommy, I learned to count to 70 in Spanish. So, one day during class, I confidently raised my hand, and when Mrs. Towes called on me, I stood up and immediately proceeded to count to 70 in Spanish before either she or my teacher Miss (no Ms. back then) Dixon could stop me. The amazement on their faces was Mastercard priceless. When I sat

down, all of my classmates were kinda hatin', so Mrs. Towes said that for my extra credit she would give us all a treat during our next lesson. Well, her next visit, Mrs. Towes came in with a platter piled high with these delicious savory meat, raisin and apple filled pastry pockets called empanadas. My classmates wolfed them down, but even then as a young foodie, I remember savoring each ingredient, the texture of the pastry, and I knew that they were deep fried. That memory stayed with me all of my life, but I never had them again. However, there was a bakery called Walter's Swiss, up the street from my home, that sold them. But for some reason, they were ALWAYS sold out so I NEVER EVER got the chance to try them. But check this out. I told my son, Marques, that I was putting a recipe for this delectable treat in my cookbook. Marques said, "Really??? Mom, I used to take my extra lunch money and buy empanadas up at the bakery all the time." And then he proceeded to tell me every ingredient that was in an empanada. I then realized that the reason I could never get an empanada from the local bakery was because my son was buying them up. So…it was destined that this recipe must be a part of my cookbook.

INGREDIENTS

1 can refrigerated biscuits (for these I would use the flakey
ones, not the jumbo ones, which are too doughy) ....<$1

1 roll of loose sausage OR 1 roll of ground turkey $1

1/2 box of raisins $1

1 small diced apple...Pantry or <$1

1 packet Chili or taco powder ....<$1

Sprinkle sage & red pepper flakes $1

S&P2T

DIRECTIONS

▶ Brown the sausage and season well. Depending on sausage, you
may not need much oil in pan

▶ Remove from heat and drain. Let cool slightly

▶ Fold apple and raisins into meat mixture so that all of the ingredients will be in each individual empanada

▶ Roll out the biscuit or dough (which ever one you use) to ¼
inch thick

▶ Use a biscuit cutter or a soup can to make the circle rounds
Keep in mind you will only place filling on half of the pocket

▶ Place a tbsp (based on size of your dough pieces) on half of the
biscuits rounds, fold over and crimp with fork. Be careful NOT
to over stuff or pierce dough with the fork tines

▶ Preheat oil

▶ Place empanadas into the hot oil. Turn when brown on one
side. Remove when they are browned (they will rise to the top of
the pan). This will be a short cooking time; remember, the
meat is already cooked

▶ Drain, and salt and pepper, or use any other seasoning that you
prefer, chili powder, garlic powder, onion powder, adobo, etc.

▶ For a gorgeous presentation, place on top of shredded lettuce,
and serve with salsa, (use the pineapple/peach salsa for a nice
sweet and savory combination)

Pescado Garlic Bread

Okay, call this petite snack a recipe filler, but when I walked into the grocery store and they were selling a name brand chunk light tuna, yeah it was the chunk light, not the solid albacore, for 49¢, but come on, who was I to turn my nose up? But they were also selling the same brand sardines for the same price as well. Well, on one of my cooking shows, the host uses anchovies to flavor the oil for some of the tomato sauces, so anchovies ....sardines... would this work? Heck for 49¢, I was going to find out. As I was walking through the parking lot on my way home, I thought of a kinda bruschetta appetizer. I tried it first with a marinara sauce and mozzarella cheese. Trust me, that wasn't bad. But it needed that oomph!!!! So, try this one!!!

INGREDIENTS

1-3.75 oz can of sardines, rinsed $1

1 can stewed or diced tomatoes drained or spaghetti sauce ..$1

1 diced pepperocini (hot pepper of choice) $1

2-3oz bags cheddar cheese $1

𝒟ining With the 𝒟ollar 𝒟iva

Sprinkle onion powder
(or couple tsp grated onion) ....Pantry or <$1

2 tbsp minced garlic (or garlic powder) $1

Basil, oregano, Italian seasoning $1

1/2 loaf of Italian bread or baguette,
sliced thick/diagonally ....Pantry or $1

DIRECTIONS

▶ Toast baguette slices under broiler, remove when lightly browned

▶ Lightly butter untoasted side, place peppers and tomatoes on top, place under broiler, remove when tomatoes are lightly browned

▶ Layer minced garlic, peppers and herbs over tomatoes/spaghetti sauce, S&P2T

▶ Place 1 sardine split down center, remove bones (bones may dissolve when heated)

▶ Top generously with cheddar cheese

▶ Place under broiler until cheese is melted and bubbly

▶ Sprinkle with basil. Serve immediately

Hot Queso Dip with Tomatoes & Sausage

I was introduced to this dip aloooooong time ago, but the recipe called for Velveeta® Cheese. But, as with everything nowadays, Velveeta is no longer a cheap cheese. I tried this cost effective technique. Look in the crackers and chips aisle in the $1Store, and you'll see the 8 oz plastic containers of different cheese dips, nacho, jalepeno, and cheddar cheese. Grab about 2 cheese dips of your choice and a 3-oz. bag of either cheddar or mozzarella cheese in the refrigerated section. This recipe will put in you divalicious cheese dip heaven.

INGREDIENTS

1 roll of loose sausage $1
(Original recipe didn't have sausage, but I added the sausage for sustenance.)

1 jar cheese spread $1

1 can of diced or stewed tomatoes (reserve drained liquid) ..$1

4 jalapeño slices (or you can use porcini peppers,
or pepper banana slices) $1

Crackers of choice, tortilla chips, melba toast,
triscuits, pita or pretzel chips $1

DIRECTIONS

▶ Brown sausage, season to taste (OPTIONAL: sprinkle crushed red pepper flakes) and drain well

▶ In a large microwave bowl, empty the cheese dips and the tomatoes, and jalapeño slices

▶ Microwave approx 8 minutes or until the cheese has melted completely. Stir

▶ Remove from microwave before the cheese burns around edges

▶ Fold in cooked sausage and stewed tomatoes

▶ If cheese dip is too thick, use the reserve juice from the tomatoes until desired texture is achieved. (May have to reheat

Dining With the Dollar Diva

slightly to incorporate the juice from the tomatoes)
▶ Serve with tortilla chips, melba toast, pita chips or pretzels chips, and mojitas or margaritas (oooppps, that's from another store!!!)

Divalicious Menus with Ingredients Costing $1 or Less

Joe's Chips

One of the biggest compliments that I received while writing this book was from my church member & Tuesday PM Bible Study participant Joe Sessoms. I had taken a break from the Dollar Diva cookbook and made a chicken enchilada dip. But, then I realized that I didn't have any chips to serve with the dip, and time was getting short to serve my taste testing crew. Since I was unable to run out and buy some chips/crackers, I noticed that I had a package of flour tortillas in the refrigerator that were left over from when I fried the tortilla strips for the Southwest Chili Salad. Anyway..... I put some oil in a skillet and turned the heat up, and then quickly went to work cutting a stack of 10 tortillas in half, then in half and then in half again. Man, I was wielding that knife like an Iron Chef. It didn't appear that I had enough, so I just cut the remaining chips and fried all of them. Then I started looking for some seasonings, spices, and herbs, cause even though I made these before, I needed a flavorful accompaniment with this full-bodied dip. I happened to see my ever faithful plastic lime, seasoned salt, cayenne/lemon peppers, garlic/onion powders and dried parsley. I was ready; I set up my chip draining station and dropped the tortilla chips in the hot oil. As I took each batch of chips out of the oil, I seasoned them immediately. I packed them up uncovered, so they wouldn't loose their crispiness, and took my mini banquet over to Bethel.

But let's get back to the compliment........ That following Sunday, Joe Sessoms approached me during our weekly coffee hour and asked me, "Where did you get purchase those chips? I went to Wal-Mart, Target, K-Mart, local supermarkets, gas stations, and I couldn't find them!" I politely told him that made them. He told me that they were the best tortilla chips he ever had and that I should serve them every week. When I told Ms. Patsy, she started chuckling and told me that after that week's Bible Study, Joe had stood right in front of the bowl of tortilla chips and took possession of them, barely letting anyone else have any.

Joe, this one's for you!!!

INGREDIENTS

1 package of flour tortillas...$1

1 cup oil $1/Pantry

Seasonings and herbs of your choice...........................Pantry

DIRECTIONS

▶ Place oil into a large skillet on medium high heat

▶ Stack as many tortillas as possible and cut in half 3 times, producing 8 chips per tortilla

▶ When oil is hot, carefully place chips in oil. May have to reduce heat to prevent burning

▶ Remove when chips rise up to top of oil. Keep eye on them as they cook fast

▶ Place chips on a paper towel to drain the oil off, and season immediately

Cheese Fondue

This recipe is a chic take off of the queso dip. Nice to serve for those special guests.

INGREDIENTS

1 8-oz jar jalapeno cheese dip $1
1/2 can evaporated milk or heavy cream (may use more
   depending upon your desired thickness) ....<$1
1 bag scallops..$1
1 bag shrimp $1
1 smoked sausage ....10-4-$10
1 bag cubed ham $1
2 hot dogs $1
1 package skewers $1

DIRECTIONS

▶ Preheat double boiler on medium high heat
▶ Put cheese dip and evaporated milk or heavy cream in a saucepan/bowl and place on heat
▶ Put dippers on skewers. Dippers could be croutons, scallops, shrimp, cubed ham, hot dogs, smoked sausages, etc.
▶ Reduce heat, stir constantly until cheese is smooth sauce
▶ Pour into serving bowl
▶ Serve immediately

Sausage Pinwheels

No story here, this is just a really good tasty treat that I'm sure you'll enjoy. You can cut the pinwheels smaller for hors d'oeuvre size or measure la for a truly satisfying snack when you need something more substantial to nibble on. You can use either refrigerated biscuit/crescent or pizza dough. It's your call. Topping the pinwheels with marinara sauce or cheese is a nice compliment for this savory divalicious treat.

INGREDIENTS

2 cans refrigerated biscuits or pizza dough $1

1 roll loose sausage $1

8-oz frozen spinach (drained) $1

2 tbsp onion/onion flakes $1

2 tbsp minced garlic $1

8-oz cottage cheese (small curd) $1

3 oz mozzarella cheese ....$1 or 10-4-$10

3 oz cheddar cheese ....$1 or 10-4-$10

4 strips roasted/marinated red peppers-diced $1

2 tbsp sage, rosemary, basil $1

DIRECTIONS

▶ Preheat oven to 350-degrees, lightly grease baking dish

▶ Brown sausage, S&P2T, drain off oil

▶ Mix cottage, mozzarella and cheddar cheeses together, S&P2T, add minced garlic, and seasonings

▶ Fold spinach (make sure it's well-drained, and squeeze out additional water) and roasted peppers into cheese mixture

▶ Roll out dough of your choice on floured wax paper surface

▶ Spread a layer of the cheese & spinach mixture on dough, leaving a ½ on lengthwise edge

▶ Tightly roll lengthwise, using wax paper to wrap, and put in freezer for 10 minutes. This will make it easier for you to cut (suggest using a serrated knife)

▶ Remove from freezer, cut into 2" rolls, and place in LIGHTLY greased baking dish. Rolls will rise and spread

▶ Cook for approximately 25 minutes, or until dough inside pinwheel is cooked though

▶ Let sit for approximately 5 minutes. Then serve.

$1 Diva FYI

$ Strongly suggest reheating in conventional oven vs microwave.

$ If you prefer a thinner/crunchier crust, use regular biscuit dough.

Mini Quiches

Many, many years ago during the "cable years", (I had to cut it back, or it cut me back—I had Marques' college tuition to pay), I got hooked watching the FoodNetwork, as did ALL of America!!! I belong to a group called The Sterling, where each member has to host a meeting in her home (or at the church, if this tidbit of info has already been discussed previously, forgive me, I'm middle-aged, and we do tend to repeat ourselves.) It was my time to impress, I mean hold "club meeting", and I was going to have my usual salmon, but I needed a few WOW hors d'oeuvres that would be delicious, but on the cheap, if you know what I mean. I couldn't think of anything, so WWSLM (What would Sandra Lee Make???). And I immediately thought of mini-quiches (for my first introduction to quiches check out my next book!! How's that for a shameless plug!!!). Anyway, always willing to give credit where credit is due, I'm not sure if this is one of Sandra Lee's Semi-Homemade recipes, but once again, my refrigerated biscuits came to the rescue for this quick, fast, easy and inexpensive WOW appetizer. Now, the first time I used ground turkey. However, there are so many other accoutrements that I noticed in the $1 Store that I've used since then.

INGREDIENTS
1 roll refrigerated biscuits (use the flakey ones for a thinner crust)

6 eggs $1

1/2 c milk (optional)..$1

1 cup shredded cheese of your choice ....$1 or 10-4-$10

1/4 tsp baking powder (optional) ....Pantry or $1

1/4 tsp nutmeg ....Pantry or $1

S2YT taste dried herbs~basil, parsley, Italian seasonings, oregano ....Pantry or $1

DIRECTIONS
▶ Preheat oven to 350 degrees

▶ Lightly spray/grease muffin tins

- Use the larger muffin size if you are serving as an entrée. If this is an appetizer, I suggest you use the smaller size muffin tin.
- I would not recommend using paper muffin cups. I would use the foil ones for a nice presentation, but the quiches will be okay if you don't use them.

▶ Separate biscuits

▶ Split each biscuit in half and roll out to 1/4" thickness

▶ Biscuit should be rolled out to be slightly larger than the muffin tin

▶ Place biscuit crusts in individual muffin tins

▶ In a mixing bowl, whisk eggs w/milk until mixture becomes light yellow

▶ S&P2T

▶ Pour egg mixture into prepared quiche crusts, fill until ¾ full, as egg mixture will rise slightly

▶ Cook approximately 10-15 minutes for the smaller muffin tins, or 15-20 minutes for the larger muffin tins, or until quiches are firm in center

▶ Remove from oven and sprinkle with extra shredded cheese or parsley

▶ Serve hot, warm or cool

▶ Okay to make ahead of time, and you can freeze it for later use

$1 Diva FYI

$ Adding spinach, broccoli, sausage, shrimp, scallops, tilapia, salmon, ground beef or sausage are delicious quiche alternatives.

Dipping Sauces

For each recipe, put all ingredients together in a small bowl and mix throughly.

Chipolte-Wasabi Mayonnaise

1/2 c mayonnaise ....Pantry or $1
1/4 c horseradish ....Pantry or $1
1 tsp crushed red pepper flakes...........................Pantry or $1
2 tsp hot sauce ....Pantry or $1
1 tsp chipolte peppers ....Pantry or $1
1 tsp wasabi ....Pantry or $1

Dijon Mayonnaise

1/2 cup mayonnaise ....Pantry or $1
1/2 cup sour cream..Pantry or $1
3 tbsp Dijon mustard ....Pantry or $1
Minced garlic/garlic powder ....Pantry or $1
Onion flakes ....Pantry or $1
1/4 c roasted peppers ....Pantry or $1

Prickly Relish

1/2 cup relish...Pantry or $1
1/4 cup pepperonci peppers ....Pantry or $1

Curry Mayonnaise

1/2 c mayonnaise ....Pantry or $1
1/4 cup spicy brown mustard ....Pantry or $1
1 tsp curry powder ....Pantry or $1
1/4 tsp cumin ....Pantry or $1
Red pepper flakes ....Pantry or $1

Spicy Blue Cheese Dipping Sauce

1/2 cup blue cheese dressing ....Pantry or $1
1 tsp crushed red pepper flakes ....Pantry or $1
1/2 cup mayonnaise ....Pantry or $1
1/4 cup feta cheese ....Pantry or $1

Dill Sauce

1/2 cup Mayonnaise ....Pantry or $1
1/2 cup sour cream ....Pantry or $1
3 tbsp minced garlic ....Pantry or $1
1/4 cup dill ....Pantry or $1

Spicy Ketchup

1 cup ketchup ....Pantry or $1
3 tbsp garlic ....Pantry or $1
2 tsp hot sauce ....Pantry or $1
1 tsp minced pepperocini peppers ....Pantry or $1
1/2 tsp sugar ....Pantry or $1

Marmalade Mayonnaise

1/2 c mayonnaise ....Pantry or $1
1/4 orange marmalade ....Pantry or $1
1/4 tsp red pepper flakes ....Pantry or $1
SP2T ....Pantry or $1

Spicy Mayo

2 tbsp red pepper flakes ....Pantry or $1
1/2 c mayo ....Pantry or $1
1/4 c ketchup ....Pantry or $1
2 tbsp hot sauce ....Pantry or $1

Notes

Divalicious Menus with Ingredients Costing $1 or Less

Notes

_____

_____

_____

_____

_____

_____

_____

_____

_____

_____

_____

_____

_____

_____

_____

_____

_____

_____

_____

_____

_____

_____

_____

_____

_____

Divalicious Menus with Ingredients Costing $1 or Less

2

Burgers, Sandwiches, & Paninis

Divalicious Menus with Ingredients Costing $1 or Less

Burgers, Sandwiches, & Paninis

$1Diva Tips

$ Purchase day old breads and rolls. Good bargains and day old breads are excellent for grilled, and toasted sandwiches and paninis.

$ For late night snacks, make a half of a sandwich or mini burgers.

$ Use the dipping sauces for toppings on your sandwiches.

$ Check out your local bakery outlets. They sell breads and rolls for $1 or less.

$ For feeding a crowd, make mini burgers or mini chicken sandwiches and use dinner rolls as buns.

$ Try using soy sauce, Worcestershire sauce or balsamic vinegar instead of salt.

$ The sandwich recipes are for a single serving. But you know how much you want on your sandwich, right? So there may not be any measurements, but if you are making more than one serving, then increase accordingly.

$ Be careful when toasting with your waffle iron. It is not necessary to press down on the waffle iron because the filling may fall out of the sandwich bread.

$ For easy clean-ups, mix your egg wash and dredging ingredients in separate lidded containers.

$1 Store Lobster Rolls

My current Pastor, Rev. Carlos Bounds, and his family vacationed on Cape Cod/Martha's Vineyard for a week this past summer. Rev. Bounds said that he intended on just kicking back, relaxing, and eating lobster rolls. Then the light bulb went off. The next morning I went to my friendly dollar store to purchase the below ingredients and prayed that the recipe "tasted like a good idea". I made two versions, first following the true lobster roll recipe. The second adaptation was my jacked up one (similar verbiage to Emeril Lagasse's "kicked up a notch" phrase). Both were and are quite tasty.

INGREDIENTS

1 package imitation seafood/lobster	10-4-$10 or $1
1-3 oz bag of shrimp (peeled and thawed)	10-4-$10 or $1
1-3 oz bag of scallops	10-4-$10 or $1
1/2 c mayonnaise	Pantry or $1
2 tsp horseradish sauce	Pantry or $1
2 tsp dijon mustard	Pantry or $1

Divalicious Menus with Ingredients Costing $1 or Less

1/2 c sour cream ....Pantry or $1
S2YT fresh/dried dill ....Pantry or $1
S&P2T
1 tbsp butter ....Pantry or $1
1 pack of 8 hot dog buns ....Pantry or $1
shredded lettuce ....Pantry or Produce Market

DIRECTIONS

▶ Preheat lightly greased skillet

▶ Cut the lobster meat into bite sized chunks

▶ Saute imitation lobster, shrimp and scallops in pan until opaque. Remove from heat so they won't over cook, and drain on paper towel

▶ Mix mayonnaise, sour cream, dijon mustard, peppers and horseradish sauce together with dry dill

▶ Fold shrimp, scallops and lobster/seafood into mayonnaise mixture

▶ Toast hot dog roll and spread lightly with butter. Line with shredded lettuce

▶ Fill with "lobster" salad

$1 Diva FYI

$ For the "jacked up" version, add red pepper flakes and diced hot peppers of your choice.

$ Adjust mayonnaise and sour cream to your desired creaminess.

Panini Waffle Sandwiches and Quesadillas

Panini are all the rage now, but what do ya do if you don't have a panini maker? You use a George Foreman grill. Well, what if you don't own a George Foreman grill? You use a waffle iron. What do you use if you don't have a quesadillo iron? You use a waffle iron. Like I've said before, you have to be resourceful when cooking!!!! So this section will be reserved for sandwiches and quesadillos. Using a waffle iron gives a new look to the classic grilled cheese sandwiches and these new kids on the block as well.

Strawberry Preserves & Cheese

My editor and publisher put me through the ringer for ingredients amounts, but come on, these are sandwiches. If you have the appropriate ingredient, then you'll be able to make these intriguingly divalicious sandwiches.

INGREDIENTS

Strawberry Preserves $1

Mozzarella or Monterey Jack cheese
(use a good melting cheese)..................................10-4-$10

Dried Basil/Fresh $1

Butter/Margarine ....Pantry

Pumpernickel bread sliced thick, but any whole wheat,
multi-grain bread will be a good substitute......................$1

Cinnamon sugar and nutmeg ....Pantry or $1

DIRECTIONS

▶ Preheat panini/Foreman grill/waffle iron

▶ Butter one side of each slice of pumpernickel bread and lightly grease panini, turn buttered side face down on cutting board

▶ Spread the strawberry preserves on both sides of bread and sprinkle the basil. If you have fresh basil, feel free to use it

▶ Slice cheese thick and use one slice of cheese per sandwich

▶ Sprinkle with cinnamon sugar and nutmeg

▶ Put both pieces of sandwich together and place on a lightly greased waffle iron. Close the waffle iron

▶ When sandwich has a nice crust, remove, cut in quarters and eat immediately

$1 Diva FYI

$ Substitute strawberry preserves with blackberry preserves or orange marmalade or apricot preserves.

Monte Cristo

INGREDIENTS
    1 container sliced turkey
    (in dollar store refrigerated section) $1
    2-3 slices (per sandwich) ham, bacon, salami $1
    1 loaf sour dough bread
    (remember to check the day old bread section) $1
    Cheese of your choice
    (use a good melting cheese)..........................$1 or 10-4-$10
    Strawberry, blackberry, raspberry jam or preserves
    (optional) $1
    Powdered sugar (optional) $1
    Batter:
        1 c flour..Pantry or $1
        1 tsp baking powder ....Pantry or $1
        1 c milk ....Pantry or $1
        1 egg ....Pantry or $1

DIRECTIONS
▶ Preheat waffle iron, grease lightly with butter or margarine

▶ Make sandwich(es) first, then place on your cooking surface

▶ Mix all ingredients for batter in a flat bottom dish where you
can dip the sandwiches

▶ Take a sandwich at a time and dip/coat both sides in the batter

▶ Place sandwich on waffle iron and then close, pressing down
slightly

▶ Microwave preserves/jam until it's syrupy

▶ Remove when sandwich has a nice crust and cheese is melted

▶ Cut into triangles, sprinkle with powdered sugar

▶ Pour fruit syrup into a small bowl and use for dipping the sandwich.

$1DIVA FYI

$ Can use a skillet to make this sandwich.

Peanut Butter & Bananas w/Honey

INGREDIENTS

Whole wheat bread $1

Peanut Butter $1

Banana sliced thin ....<$1

Cinnamon sugar $1

Honey..$1

Butter/Margerine ....Pantry or $1

DIRECTIONS

▶ Lightly butter one side of each slice of whole wheat bread and sprinkle buttered side with cinnamon sugar. Turn face down on cutting board

▶ Spread peanut butter on both sides of bread

▶ Top one slice with the banana slices and sprinkle with a dash of cinnamon sugar

▶ Put both pieces of sandwich together and place on a lightly greased waffle iron. Close

▶ When sandwich has browned, remove, cut into half and drizzle with honey. Eat immediately

Hardboiled Western Omelet & Cheddar Cheese Sandwich

INGREDIENTS

Hardboiled egg-sliced ....$1 or <$1

1 can of chunk ham or sliced ham diced $1

½ cup frozen onions and peppers $1

¼ c marinated mushrooms sliced $1

¼ c shredded cheddar cheese $1

1 tbsp butter/margerine ....Pantry or $1

Baguette sliced thick $1

DIRECTIONS

▶ Preheat waffle iron

▶ Heat skillet to med high, melt butter or margarine

▶ Saute your onions, peppers and mushrooms in a hot skillet

▶ Butter one side of each slice of bread, turn buttered side face down on cutting board

▶ Place one half of cheese and ham on top unbuttered side of bread

▶ Place sliced egg, onions, peppers and mushroom on top of the ham, S&P2T

▶ Layer remaining cheese on top, top with 2nd slice of bread

▶ Place sandwich on greased waffle iron, then close

▶ Remove when sandwich has a nice brown crust and cheese is melted

▶ Cut in half and serve immediately

- -

$1DIVA FYI

$ Entire sandwich can be made using a skillet instead of cooking sandwich on your waffle iron.

- -

Cinnamon Apple—Almond Raisin Waffle Panini

INGREDIENTS

4 slices whole wheat bread $1

1 jar apples (drained) $1/1 fresh apple if available, thinly sliced

Raisins $1

Sprinkle cinnamon & nutmeg..$1

Sprinkle brown sugar...$1

Almond (crushed). If your $1 Store doesn't carry them, check out your local drugs stores — they usually carry the pocket size nuts, like macadamia, almonds, hazelnut, etc

Butter/margerine ....Pantry or <$1

DIRECTIONS

▶ Lightly butter both sides of each slice of wheat bread

▶ Sprinkle each slice of bread with cinnamon, nutmeg, and brown sugar

▶ Layer thinly sliced apple slices on one slice of bread and sprinkle raisins and almonds over the apples

▶ Sprinkle cinnamon and/or nutmeg and brown sugar on top of the apples, almonds and raisins.

▶ Top with 2nd slice of bread

▶ Place sandwich in waffle iron and close

▶ When sandwich has a nice crust, remove, cut in quarters and eat immediately

$1 Diva FYI

$ The fresh apples will have a nice crunch to them.

$ Substitue raisins with dried cranberries and substitute almonds with walnuts, if available.

Mc$1 Store Breakfast Sandwich

INGREDIENTS

4 frozen waffles $1

2 slices Pork Roll or loose sausage $1

4 eggs $1

SP2T...Pantry

Splash of milk ....Pantry

½ cup Cheese dip $1

1 tbsp margarine ....Pantry

DIRECTIONS

▶ Preheated oven to 425 degrees to brown waffles or use toaster

▶ Preheat lightly greased skillet on medium heat, when hot, brown slice of pork roll and remove from skillet OR

▶ Make sausage patties the size of waffle and fry in skillet until done

▶ Beat eggs and add a splash of milk, S&P2T

▶ Preheat clean skillet on medium heat melt shortening (do not allow to brown). Reduce heat to low

▶ Pour in scrambled eggs, stir constantly,

▶ Microwave cheese dip to a smooth creamy consistency, if too thick, add splash of milk

▶ Butter 1 side of each waffle

▶ Place slice of pork roll/sausage on one waffle

▶ Top pork roll/sausage with scrambled eggs

▶ Pour melted cheese sauce over eggs

▶ Top with remaining waffle

$DIVA FYI:

$ Substitute poached or fried eggs for scrambled eggs.

$ Substitute waffles with bagels or English muffins.

Shrimp and Scallop Quesadilla

INGREDIENTS

2 tortillas...$1

1-4 oz bag shrimp – thawed $1

1-3 oz bag scallop - thawed $1

1-3 oz bag cheddar cheese $1

¼ c stir fry onions & peppers $1

2 pepperoncini peppers sliced $1

DIRECTIONS

▶ Preheat skillet on medium heat

▶ Preheat another pan on medium high, with oil to sauté seafood, onions and peppers

▶ Sauté the shrimp, scallops, stir fry onions, peppers and the pepperoncini on the waffle iron

▶ When the seafood is pink around edges it is cooked, remove

▶ Place one tortilla in the heated pan

▶ Layer shrimp, scallops, onions, and both peppers on one tortilla and top with cheese

▶ Place 2nd tortilla on top

▶ Carefully flip tortilla over to the other side

▶ Remove quesadilla when cheese is melted and tortillas are soft and warm

▶ Cut into 8 equal pieces and serve with salsa and sour cream

$DIVA FYI

$ Substitute the shrimp and/or scallops with either chunk tuna, chunk ham, chunk chicken, tilapia, flounder, or salmon.

Chicken Sliders (Mini Chicken Sandwiches)

I ran into a fellow $1 Store colleague/shopper during one of my many visits and I noticed that she was checking out with about ten bags of chicken tenders. Being the snob that I am, I've always made my own chicken tenders and I never even looked twice the chicken strips/tenders, nuggets and popcorn chicken the $1 Store's refrigerated section. I asked her what was she going to do with 10 bags of chicken tenders. She advised me that she was hosting a tea for the senior women members of her church. She said that she planned on serving the chicken strips on a beautiful silver platter and piercing them with pretty colored cellophane tipped toothpicks and accompanying them with various dipping sauces, blue cheese, honey mustard, barbecue, etc. Hmmmmm….. that got me to thinking, what other ways could I serve these $1 Store chicken tenders? Suddenly Chili's commercial for chicken sliders came to mind.

INGREDIENTS

1 bag chicken breast strips (approximately 8 tenders per bag)....$1
1 pkg hot dog rolls $1
Dill pickle chips...$1

DIRECTIONS

▶ Heat pan of oil to fry tenders (okay to bake, but frying brings out flavor)

▶ S&P2T immediately after removing from oil while draining

▶ Open hotdog rolls, cut rolls in half crosswise and place under broiler, remove when toasted

▶ Spread spicy mayonnaise on one side of each roll and put pickles on the other half of the roll
▶ Put 1 chicken tender on each roll (top with a little bit of shredded lettuce)
▶ Pierce w/toothpick to keep slider together
▶ Arrange on platter and serve immediately

$1 Store Po' Boy

You've probably already read my previous $1 Store lobster roll recipe. But while I was shopping for the lobster roll ingredients, I kept looking at the smoked oysters on the shelves and wondered what, besides my oyster

dressing and Mrs. Smalls scrumptious escalloped oysters (which would probably be >$1), I could make. Then the light bulb went off. Even though lobster rolls are a New England specialty, with this recipe you'll travel to the French Quarter for this lip smacking Creole tasty delight.

INGREDIENTS

1 package seafood/imitation crab legs $1
1-3 oz bags shrimp (peeled) $1
1-3 oz bags scallops $1
1 can smoked oysters $1
1 egg $1
¼ c milk ....Pantry or $1
½ c flour ....Pantry or $1
½ c seasoned bread crumbs ....<$1
S2YT seafood seasoning, Old Bay, or crab seasoning............$1
1 c vegetable/corn oil ....Pantry or $1
1 pack 8 hot dog rolls $1
1 tbsp softened butter/margarine ....Pantry or $1

DIRECTIONS

▶ Preheat pan with oil

▶ Beat egg and milk

▶ Dredge all seafood in egg & milk mixture

▶ Pour flour, bread crumbs and seasonings in a paper bag or plastic container with lid

▶ S&P2T

▶ Place egg coated seafood in the paper bag or bowl and shake. (Don't put all of the seafood in at one time as it will clump and will not coat seafood evenly.)

▶ Carefully place seafood in the hot oil, fry until brown, S&P2T as soon as you take out of oil and then drain. You may have to cook several batches

▶ Spread a light layer of butter on roll and toast, then line with shredded lettuce

▶ Fill with fried seafood. Top with chipolte mayonnaise.

▶ Serve immediately

$1 Sausage & Peppers Burgers

Now the folks from the various Jersey shores boast of having the best sausage and peppers. Bottom line — there is nothing like a burger. So, I thought that I would devote a couple of recipes to a variety of extraordinary types of burgers.

INGREDIENTS

1 roll loose sausage, thawed	$1
Roll of ground turkey	$1
1-8 oz bag stir fried onions and peppers	$1
1 cup meatless spaghetti sauce	$1
Dried basil/fresh basil	Pantry or Produce Market
2 tbsp minced garlic	Pantry or $1
1 tbsp cooking oil	Pantry or $1
Hamburger rolls	$1
2 tbsp Worchestershire sauce	Pantry or $1
1 tbsp balsamic vinegar	Pantry or $1

DIRECTIONS

▶ Preheat large skillet at medium temp

▶ Add cooking oil, and sauté onions and peppers, SP2T until slightly carmelized, and then remove from pan

▶ Mix ground turkey and sausage and add 1 tbsp minced garlic, Worcestershire sauce, and balsamic vinegar, SP2T

▶ Score mixture into 6 sections, then shape sausage into burgers and place into pan (don't overcrowd pan. You may have to cook 2 burgers at a time)

▶ After shaping burgers, use your thumb to make an indention in te center of one side of the burger. This depression will allow for even cooking of your burger and prevent the burger from swelling.

▶ Increase pan temp to med-high. You may/may not need to

add additional oil as some sausages may contain more fat than others.

▶ Cook sausage burgers 4 minutes on each side, then remove from pan

▶ Pour off excess oil, and then deglaze pan with spaghetti sauce and remaining minced garlic, add basil, SP2T. Then place the peppers, onions and burgers back into the spaghetti sauce.

▶ Simmer uncovered for 5 minutes

▶ Place burger and peppers & onions on hamburger rolls

▶ Serve hot

$1DIVA FYI

$ If after scoring meat and the hamburgers are too large for your tastes, make them to your desired size. Then take the remaining sausage burger mixture and measure into the size burgers that are satisfactory to you. Roll into balls and place into a freezer bag. This way you can thaw out a burger(s) as needed.

Dining With the Dollar Diva

Inside-out Cheeseburgers

INGREDIENTS

1 roll sausage $1

1 roll ground turkey $1

4 slices of the cheese of your choice ......Pantry, 10-4$10 or $1

4 hamburger rolls $1

1 tsp each Worcestershire sauce, soy sauce and
balsalmic vinegar ....Pantry or $1

DIRECTIONS

▶ Preheat oven to 350 degrees

▶ Cut cheese

▶ Mix ground turkey, sausage and Worcestershire sauce , soy
sauce and balsamic vinegar together in a mixing bowl

▶ Section the meat mixture into the number of burgers you desire

▶ Make indent in center of each burger with your thumb

▶ Divide shredded cheese equally for the number of burgers you
are making

▶ Place cheese into the indentation, then reshape burger around
the cheese filling

▶ Shape hamburgers, making a dent in center

▶ S&P2T

▶ Place on greased bak-
ing sheet, and bake in
oven until cooked to
your liking

▶ Set for 2 minutes, top
with your favorite buns
and toppings

Divalicious Menus with Ingredients Costing $1 or Less

Salsa Burgers

INGREDIENTS
1 roll ground turkey $1
1 roll sausage $1
1/4 c salsa $1
1/2 c bread crumbs..$1
Hamburger rolls $1
1 tsp each Worchestershire sauce, soy sauce and balsalmic
  vinegar ....Pantry or <$1
S&P2T ....Pantry
Cheese optional

DIRECTIONS
▶ Preheat oven to 350 degrees

▶ Mix turkey and sausage, breadcrumbs and salsa together.

▶ Add Worcestershire sauce, soy sauce and balsamic vinegar.

▶ Section the meat mixture into the number of burgers you desire

▶ Shape hamburgers. Make indent in center of each burger with your thumb

▶ Place on greased baking sheet, and bake in oven until cooked to your liking

▶ Set for 2 minutes. Top with cheese (optional) or your favorite buns and toppings

Dining With the Dollar Diva

Meatball Subs

INGREDIENTS

1 bag meatballs $1

1 jar/can spaghetti sauce..$1

1 c stir fry onions and peppers $1

1 jar/can mushrooms, drained ....Pantry or <$1

1 tsp each Worcestershire sauce, soy sauce and
  balsalmic vinegar ....Pantry or $1

S&P2T

2 tbsp sugar (I've used a sugar substitute and it works just fine)

1 tsp each of basil, oregano, and/or Italian seasonings $1

½ c oil ....Pantry or $1

2 tbsp chopped garlic.......................................Pantry or $1

1 pack hamburger, hot dog, or dinner rolls ......$1 or 10-4-$10

Cheese optional

DIRECTIONS

▶ Preheat saucepan with oil, reserve 2 tbsp

▶ Place meatballs in oil, brown then remove. S&P2T

▶ In a separate saucepan place remaining oil. Heat and
  caramelize stir fry onions, peppers and mushrooms

▶ Pour in spaghetti sauce

▶ Add remaining ingredients (including meatballs) and bring to
  a simmering boil, stirring sauce when necessary to prevent
  burning

▶ Lower heat, cover and
  let simmer for 15 min-
  utes

▶ Place on rolls and top
  with cheese of your
  choice

▶ Serve

Notes

_____

_____

_____

_____

_____

_____

_____

_____

_____

_____

_____

_____

_____

_____

_____

_____

_____

_____

_____

_____

_____

_____

_____

_____

Dining With the Dollar Diva

Notes

Divalicious Menus with Ingredients Costing $1 or Less

Notes

_____

_____

_____

_____

_____

_____

_____

_____

_____

_____

_____

_____

_____

_____

_____

_____

_____

_____

_____

_____

_____

_____

_____

Dining With the Dollar Diva

Divalicious Menus with Ingredients Costing $1 or Less

3

Main Course Entrées

Divalicious Menus with Ingredients Costing $1 or Less

Main Course Entrées

$Diva Tips

$ If you have time, browse around your local supermarkets for in-store specials.

$ Take time to window shop at food stores that you don't regularly patronize. You may be pleasingly surprised at the bargains that you've been missing out on.

$ If you find those bargains that you cannot pass on, remember, FREEZE, FREEZE, FREEZE.

$ When browning sausage, you may not need to add additional oil, depending upon the sausage's fat content.

Ms. Branda's Shepherd's Pie

As luck would have it, my local grocery store has the refrigerated biscuits on sale 10 for $10. Mmmmm.....let's see what quick and delicious recipes I can come up with. And low and behold, shepherd's pie came to mind. I remember back in 1988, my cousin Melvie and his family were living with me, and all four of us, Melvie, his wife Dee-Dee, their son Justin and I, caught this horrible flu virus. We all went down for the count for approximately two days, but what we all later found to be hilarious was that we never lost our appetites. We ate the entire time. My mother brought us gallons of orange juice and humongous bags of apples like she had just picked them from the orchard. Ms. Branda, Dee-Dee's mother, called and asked if we needed anything special, like cough syrup, aspirin, antihistamine, etc. Dee-Dee told her that she wanted a shepherd's pie. And before we knew it, Ms. Branda was knocking at the door with this picture perfect meat and vegetable-filled pastry topped with the fluffiest mashed potatoes. I couldn't eat it, not because I wasn't feeling well, but because it was beef. If she had done a chicken one, I woulda been all over it.

INGREDIENTS

1 roll ground beef/turkey $1
1 roll ground sausage $1
16 oz frozen mixed vegetables/2 cans vegetables (drained) ..$1
1 pack instant potatoes $1
¼ cup flour ....Pantry or $1
½ cup broth ....Pantry or <$1
4 tbsp butter/margarine ....Pantry or $1
¼ cup frozen stir fried onions and peppers $1
2 tbsp minced garlic...$1
1 c milk ....Pantry or <$1

DIRECTIONS

▶ Preheat oven to 325 degrees
▶ Arrange biscuits on a floured surface and roll thin enough for

the baking dish you are using
- ▶ Place into baking dish and crimp dough around the dish edge
- ▶ Bake crust for approximately ½ cooking time, then remove from oven. Press crust down.
- ▶ In a medium high sauce pan, melt the butter, and stir in garlic and onion, peppers and onions, sauté until translucent
- ▶ Add ground beef and sausage, and brown
- ▶ Sprinkle flour over meat mixture and stir
- ▶ Stir in ½ cup broth and add vegetables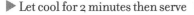
- ▶ Let simmer on a low heat
- ▶ Pour ground beef/turkey, allow meat mixture to thicken. Add sausage and vegetables into pie crust
- ▶ Prepare mashed potatoes according to the package directions
- ▶ Top pie with mashed potatoes, and place under broiler until potatoes are browned
- ▶ Let cool for 2 minutes then serve

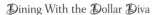

$1 Store Ravioli Carbonara

I was singing in the alto section for the Annual Main Line Black Interdenominational Ministerial Alliance Revival while a few recipes literally came to me from heaven during the worship service. So when the Revivalist was feeding my soul, God blessed me with a few recipes to feed the masses. When prayers go up, God's blessings and a few recipes come down. And this one I've been told is truly divalicious.

INGREDIENTS

1-16 oz bag of ravioli $1

2 tsp butter/margarine/olive oil ....Pantry or $1

½ cup milk OR heavy cream ....Pantry or $1

8-oz jar of white extra sharp cheese dip $1

1 tbsp chopped/minced garlic...$1

2 c shredded muenster cheese ....10-4-$10

8-oz pack of pork roll (diced) $1
S2YT basil, oregano, or Italian seasoning ....Pantry or $1
Pinch of nutmeg ....Pantry or $1

DIRECTIONS

▶ Preheat lightly greased skill on medium high heat

▶ Dice pork roll. Brown until crispy but chewy and drain off the oil

▶ Cook ravioli according to directions printed on bag

▶ Place garlic, butter and milk in saucepan on medium heat

▶ When butter is melted and milk comes to a simmer, add cheese dip and garlic, melt cheese on low heat, stir often to prevent scorching

▶ S&P2T

▶ Stir the muenster cheese and add nutmeg into the cheese sauce

▶ Drain ravioli and put in serving bowl or platter. Continue to stir until cheese has completely melted into a smooth sauce

▶ Fold pork roll into cheese sauce and pour over ravioli

▶ Sprinkle herbs over ravioli carbonara and serve

$1 Diva FYI

$ I felt that ravioli made a nicer presentation and the pork roll was a bit tastier, but feel free to use any pasta or bacon bits that is available at the $1 Store.

$ Also try this one with shrimp and scallops. Absolutely divine!!!!

A little somethin'-somethin' to go with the Pork Roll Carbonara is on the next page...

$1 Store Garlic Cheese Bread

INGREDIENTS

1 package Texas toast $1

3 tbsp minced garlic ....Pantry or $1

3/4 c mozzarella cheese ....Pantry or $1

1 tsp S2YT basil, oregano, or Italian seasoning $1

DIRECTIONS

▶ Place 6 slices of the Texas Toast® on a baking sheet

▶ Top with equal amounts of minced garlic and mozzarella cheese

▶ Sprinkle on desired Italian seasonings and S&P2T

▶ Place in oven preheated to 375 degrees. Remove when cheese browns

Cream Tomato Soup with Collard Greens & Blackbeans

I've always been a big fan of cream of tomato soup. One of the Fisher family's favorite lunches when we were home sick was American grilled cheese sandwich and condensed cream of tomato soup (we used milk instead of water). But as I matured, my taste buds required more epicurean cheeses and a creamy flavorful and robust soup. So my youthful dining habits became a tad bit upscale. Anyway… here's my adult spin take on a childhood memory.

INGREDIENTS

1-28 oz can whole tomatoes $1
1-14 oz can vegetable broth (okay to use chicken) ......Pantry or $1
1 c frozen collard greens, thawed and drained $1

Dining With the Dollar Diva

1 can black beans (rinse to keep the red color) ......Pantry or $1
½ c milk (evaporated milk makes it creamier) ....Pantry or $1
3 tbsp butter/margarine....................................Pantry or $1
2 tbsp flour ....Pantry
1 tsp sugar ....Pantry
1 tsp minced garlic..Pantry
¼ tsp nutmeg, cinnamon ....Pantry or $1
SP2T...Pantry
½ tsp basil, parsley or oregano ....Pantry or $1

DIRECTIONS

▶ Melt 2 tbsp butter/margarine in a medium saucepan
▶ Stir in flour to make roux
▶ Pour chicken/vegetable broth into roux
▶ Add garlic when mixture thickens reduce heat
▶ Pour entire can of whole tomatoes into blender
▶ Pulse tomatoes to your desired consistency
▶ Pour tomato mixture into saucepan
▶ Add collard greens and black beans to sauce pan
▶ Stir in milk
▶ Season with sugar and spices
▶ SP2T
▶ Cover sauce pan and let simmer for 20 minutes; do not boil
▶ Remove from heat
▶ Garnish with cheese and croutons

$1 Diva FYI

$ Check out the Paninis, Sandwiches and Burger section of this book or serve with your favorite grilled cheese sandwich. Divalicious!!!!!

Divalicious Menus with Ingredients Costing $1 or Less

Baked Eggs Florentine

I made this for my Mother for a Sunday morning breakfast before we went to our respective church worship services. Everything can be purchased at $1 Store, even the glass and ceramic ramekins.

INGREDIENTS

1 c frozen spinach –thawed and drained $1

6 eggs ....$1 or <$1

Salt/pepper/garlic powder/onion powder ....Pantry or <$1

Mozzarella cheese $1

Parsley and or paprika ....Pantry or <$1

DIRECTIONS

▶ Preheat oven to 400 degrees

▶ Microwave spinach for about 3-5 minutes, drain thoroughly

▶ Butter baking dish or ramekins

▶ Layer cooked spinach in bottom of ramekin or baking dish

▶ S&P2T and add garlic & onion powder

▶ Carefully crack open the eggs on top of the spinach

▶ Layer shredded mozzarella cheese

▶ Sprinkle with paprika

▶ Place in oven and bake for approximately 5 minutes-or until eggs are cooked to your liking.

▶ Sprinkle with fresh or dried parsley or herb of your choice

$1 Diva FYI

$ You can bake in ramekins so everyone has their own individual serving. Or you can bake in a baking dish and serve at table for a beautiful presentation.

$ Make sure that your spinach is thawed and drained thoroughly before layering in the baking dish or ramekin.

Under the Boardwalk

For a while, unbeknownst to them, Bethel Bryn Mawr's Tuesday afternoon Bible Study class was secretly chosen to be my taste testers for some of the recipes in this book. One Tuesday afternoon, I took a Pyrex® baking dish of my Dolla 'bons to our church secretary Ms. Patsy's office. I told her that I was refining the recipe and baking process and I needed her to share them with Rev. Bounds. I knew that Ms. Patsy would provide me with the solid constructive feedback; Rev. Bounds would stroke my ego and tell me that they were good, regardless. Anyway, I dropped the baking pan on her desk and she peeled back the aluminum foil, took one look and then closed her eyes. She took a deep breath, and it appeared that she actually tasted the spice laden cinnamon, nutmeg aroma that consumed the room. I flew out of the office as I knew that Bible Study would be starting soon, and I didn't want to run into any of my church members who would ask me what I was doing at the church. Remember, I was laid off about three weeks prior and didn't want to have to explain my employment situation. What I didn't know until a few days later was that Ms. Patsy had shared or HAD to share Dolla Store Cinnabons with several of the Tuesday Bible Study Class members. She told me that they were a big hit and the following Sunday, our First Lady, Sister Amy, told me that she absolutely loved them.

So......I decided that it would be a great idea to have a mini repast for the Tuesday afternoon Bible Study class and have them critically assess my dishes!!! Having a bit of Auntie Babs in me, I made sure that I had an aesthetically pleasing tablescape, because before you actually eat your food, you eat first by sight, then by smell, and lastly by taste. So I set up a table with tablecloths, flatware, cups, and, with Ms. Patsy's help, pitchers, and made sure that each dish was served on a colorful platter, or I used vibrant-hued baking dishes. Eventually the cat was let out of the bag, and most of the members knew I was fixing their afternoon snack. Since all Bible Study classes are concluded the first week of July, Ms. Patsy advised everyone that the 4th Tuesday in June would be their last repast because the following week I would be getting ready for my son Marques' birthday/Annual Cookout and wouldn't have time to put together a quick bit for them. Per Ms. Patsy, my

Divalicious Menus with Ingredients Costing $1 or Less

"taste testers" didn't take kindly to that. Even Rev. Bounds was a bit salty and said that he was sorry to see the "Bible Study Café" come to an end. Well, talk about stroking my ego, I went into overload and tried to think of a nice theme to end on. Since it was coming up on the July 4th holiday and people hit the shore, I envisioned my farewell lunch would be an "Afternoon at the Boardwalk". I prepared hot dogs with spicy sauerkraut, strawberry/lemon water ice, waffle ice cream sandwiches, pizza squares and cherry coke. Below are all of the recipes for all of the divalicious Boardwalk delicacy specialties I served that day.

Hot Dogs and Spicy Sauerkraut

INGREDIENTS

8 hot dogs/polish sausages $1

1 8oz can of sauerkraut $1

½ bag stir fry onions & peppers $1

3 tbsp red pepper flakes ....Pantry or $1

1 tsp chili powder..Pantry or $1

2 tbsp hot sauce ....Pantry or $1

3/4 c ketchup..Pantry or $1

1/4 c brown sugar..Pantry or $1

1 tbsp balsamic vinegar ....Pantry or $1

1 pack of 8 hot dog rolls ....Pantry or $1

2 tbsp oil ....Pantry or $1

3 tbsp minced garlic ....Pantry or $1

DIRECTIONS

▶ Preheat oven to 425 degrees

▶ Preheat large skillet, add oil

▶ Add sauerkraut, diced onion, ketchup and the chili pepper. S&P2T

▶ Mix well and simmer at a medium heat for approx 20 minutes.

▶ Place hot dogs/sausages on cookie sheet put in heated oven, bake until done

▶ When hot dogs are cooked, place in hot dog rolls and top with the spicy sauerkraut.

Waffle Ice Cream Sandwiches

INGREDIENTS

1 pkg frozen waffles $1

1 qt ice cream-softened -flavor of choice $1

DIRECTIONS

▶ Toast waffles according to directions printed on package (toaster or oven)

▶ Place one healthy scoop of ice cream on one waffle

▶ Place another waffle on top

▶ Repeat until you have the amount of ice cream sandwiches needed

▶ Put in freezer until time to serve

▶ If ice cream sandwiches become rock hard, allow to thaw slightly before serving

$1 Diva FYI

$ Okay the photo isn't with waffles, but every time I make waffle ice cream sandwiches, they disappear before I can take a picture.

$ If not serving immediately, wrap in wax paper and place in airtight plastic container for longer storage.

$ Be careful pressing cookies down on ice cream as you may cause the cookies to break.

Strawberry Lemon/Lime Water Ice

INGREDIENTS

1-12 oz bag frozen strawberries $1

1-12 oz can of frozen lemonade/limeade concentrate-
thawed $1

Sugar (sweeten to taste) ....Pantry or $1

Ice (don't know how much)

DIRECTIONS

▶ Place thawed lemonade concentrate and bag of strawberries,
sugar in blender

▶ Puree together

▶ Add some ice

▶ Hit button on blender that chops ice

▶ When blended sufficiently, add the remaining concentrate and
strawberries

▶ Puree

▶ Add remaining ice and hit button on blender that chops ice

▶ Pour into large container and place in freezer

$1 Diva FYI

$ To reduce freezing time, spoon water ice into the cups that you
are going to serve the water ice in.

$ Use different fruits, frozen, fresh, or canned but still use a fruit
juice concentrate as a base for extra flavor.

$ Top with fruit and a sprig of mint for a pretty presentation.

Pizza Squares

INGREDIENTS

1 can refrigerator biscuit dough (crescent rolls or flakey for a lighter crust) or pizza crust ....10-4-$10

1 cup Marina sauce...$1

2 cloves chopped garlic (garlic powder)................Pantry or $1

1 c mozzarella cheese......................................$1 or 10-4-$10

1 cup cheddar cheese ....$1 or10-4-$10

DIRECTIONS:

▶ Preheat oven to 325 degrees

▶ Roll out dough in an 11"x 9" square

▶ Mix garlic into marina sauce

▶ S&P2T

▶ Spread the marina sauce over the dough surface leaving on a 1" edge

▶ Sprinkle cheese over marina sauce

▶ Sprinkle basil, oregano, and/or Italian seasonings on pizza

▶ Place in oven for approx 20 minutes or until crust is done

▶ Set for 2 minutes

▶ Cut into squares, serve hot or warm

▶ Also see my easy calzone/stromboli recipes, for other options

$DIVA FYI

$ Top with olives, shrimp, roasted peppers, scallops, sausage, ground turkey, or extra cheese.

Cream Chicken Mushroom Corn Chowder

My oldest sister Bubbie and her two boys Colton and John stayed with me during the last two weeks of my pregnancy with Marques. One afternoon, it was just too hot to go out, and I just couldn't get comfortable. So Bubbie said "I know what you need, you need a nice bowl of cream of mushroom soup." I'm like, "whaaa da ......" The AC is set on hell and she wants be to eat some hot ass soup. But she was my big sister. I did as I was told. I ate the soup, and it was utterly delicious. All my life I always thought that cream of mushroom/celery soups were for either a base for gravy or a sauce for chicken, turkey, etc. Well that perception was proven incorrect that day. Here's one that I think you'll enjoy, even on a really hot summer day!!! Excellent comfort food.

INGREDIENTS

1 lb chicken breast or thighs	10-4-$10
1 tsp butter/margarine	Pantry or $1
2 tbsp cornstarch/flour	Pantyr or $1
1 can condensed mushroom soup	$1
1 can condensed cream of celery	$1
½ bag stir fry onions and peppers	<$1
16 oz evaporated milk	<$1
8oz can of white beans (used instead of potatoes)	<$1
8 oz canned/frozen corn	<$1
2 4oz cans mushrooms	<$1
2 tbsp minced garlic	Pantry or $1
1 c milk/1 container heavy cream	Pantry or $1

DIRECTIONS

▶ Remove skin and bones from chicken. Cut into 1 inch pieces

▶ In a large, deep saucepan, melt the butter and sauté the minced garlic, stir fry onions and peppers and mushrooms. Add chicken, cook until done

▶ Add and stir in cornstarch/flour

▶ Add evaporated milk

▶ Stir both cans of condensed cream of mushroom and celery soup into saucepan

▶ Stir in milk

▶ S&P2T

▶ Add corn and beans

▶ Cover and simmer soup at a low heat for 20 minutes

▶ Pour soup into bowls or mugs

▶ Serve hot

$1 Diva FYI

$ Garnish with herbs and croutons.

$ Swap beans with potatoes.

𝒟ining With the 𝒟ollar 𝒟iva

$1 Store Sweet & Sour Chicken/Shrimp

Years ago, while living in Washington, DC, I worked for the Potomac Electric Power Company. For years I worked the 4:15 PM-12:15 PM shift in the data entry department. I sat next to a sweet lady named Joyce, who was a mother of four children. Everyday Joyce would make dinner for her family before she came into work. So obviously, whatever Joyce made for dinner she had for "lunch" at work. Even though Joyce wasn't even ten years older than me, I became her 5th child because she always brought me lunch, too. One of my favorites was this quick and easy sweet and sour sausage/kielbasa dish she used to make almost every other week. I am thankful for this recipe that she so willingly gave to me. Unfortunately, the $1 Store doesn't sell kielbasa/smoked sausage on a regular basis (hint: stock up and freeze when you find it). However, you may find your local grocery store may do a 10-4-$10 sale. I thought that I would substitute with either chicken nuggets or the popcorn shrimp. This is a stir fry recipe, so move fast!!!

INGREDIENTS

1-6 oz bag of chicken nuggets or
14 oz box of popcorn shrimp...$1

1 c ketchup ....Pantry or $1

1-5 oz can pineapple tidbits w/heavy syrup $1

6 oz pineapple juice or orange juice.................................$1

1 tbsp vegetable oil (would not recommend butter or olive oil)

2 tbsp cornstarch ....$1 or <$1

1-6 oz bag stir fry vegetables or stir fry onions & peppers
(thawed/drained) $1

1 cup sliced carrots...$1

1-6 oz bag of frozen broccoli (drained) $1

3 tbsp hot peppers of your choice $1

4 oz can sliced mushrooms ....<$1

1 tbsp soy sauce ....Pantry or $1

S&P2T

1-16 oz package of rice (brown rice is excellent)..................$1

DIRECTIONS

▶ Cook rice according to package directions (I have a rice cooker, and it is downright fabulous)

▶ Bake or deep fry chicken nuggets or popcorn shrimp according to package directions (I prefer to fry them)

▶ Heat cooking oil of your choice in a sauce pan on medium high heat

▶ Stir fry onions and peppers, mushrooms and carrots on medium high heat

▶ Add cornstarch

▶ When vegetables become coated, add in pineapple/orange juice and stir

▶ Stir in ketchup and pineapples

▶ Season sweet and sour sauce with red pepper flakes

▶ Add soy sauce, S&P2T

▶ Let come to a simmer

▶ Add broccoli 5 minutes before serving as it will become soft/mushy and lose its bright green color

▶ Fold in chicken/shrimp to sweet and sour sauce

▶ Remove from heat

▶ Pour sweet and sour over rice

▶ Serve immediately

$1 Diva FYI

$ You can serve this sweet and sour over pasta noodles, and I suggest you use angel hair, cappellini, or vermicelli pasta noodles. If using pasta, season with a sesame seed oil and garlic and sprinkle with 2 tbsp soy sauce.

$ PS: Everyone loves fried rice, so you can modify the sweet & sour recipe. Prepare the rice according to the directions printed on the package. Stir fry your chicken and/or seafood along with your vegetables of choice. Season well with soy sauce. Grab your chopsticks, get your duck/plum sauce and hot mustard, and you're in business.

$ This is an excellent way to use leftover beef, chicken and seafood. Stretch that $1. Enjoy!!!!!

$ Try substituting the popcorn shrimp or the chicken nuggets with chicken strips.

Divalicious Menus with Ingredients Costing $1 or Less

Southwest Chili Salad

Time to hit your local produce markets or the produce section at your supermarkets. You can find alot of bargains that are good for you and good to eat. Chili (with or without beans), beans, salsa, sour cream, cheese, and hot peppers over a salad can be a meal all by itself. It's visually appealing, tasty and extremely filling. This can be served as an appetizer or entrée. It just depends on how much you make, and how many people you are serving, and your presentation. This dish can be served hot/warm or cold and is definitely a crowd pleaser. A true divalicious hit!

INGREDIENTS

1 can chili $1
2 tbsp oil ....Pantry or $1
1 can dark and/or light kidney beans, black beans ....<$1
1 can whole kernel corn (drained) ....<$1
1/2 head shredded lettuce ....Pantry or Produce Market
1 tbsp chili powder $1
1 tbsp minced garlic $1
1 tbsp parsley..$1
2 tomatoes ....Pantry or Produce Market
1 diced onion or green onions (dice the entire stalk)
....Pantry or Produce Market
1 diced pepper (of your choice) ......Pantry or Produce Market
1 c shredded cheddar cheese..$1
1 pkg or tortillas or bag of plain tortilla chips
1/2 c sour cream
1/2 c salsa $1

DIRECTIONS

▶ Preheat saucepan, add vegetable oil
▶ Cook 1/2 of onions and 1/2 peppers until translucent
▶ Stir in chili and other beans

Dining With the Dollar Diva

▶ S&P2T

▶ Add chili powder, garlic powder, your choice of seasonings

▶ Simmer

▶ Shred, rinse and dry lettuce

▶ Place in a large pasta bowl or platter

▶ Place chili & bean mixture in center of lettuce

▶ Arrange tomatoes around edge of chili & beans

▶ Put cheese on top of the chili mixture

▶ Top chili with remaining onions

▶ Then place the fried tortilla strips on top

▶ Serve with the tortillas, salsa, black olives, green chili peppers and sour cream

$DIVA FYI

$ Joe's Chips is a perfect compliment for this salad.

Calzone

I know, I know! This cookbook should be called 1,000,001 ways to use refrigerated biscuits. But food preparation is all about creativity and cooking in my kitchen allows me to be multicultural, diverse and ingenious along with being frugal. This recipe just came to me out of the blue. Believe it or not, no story behind it, I just like calzones. Try it, you'll like it! There are a couple of ways that you can go with this dish, so work with me on this one, okay? Try using vegetables, too. Just make sure that they are drained so the calzone won't be soggy.

INGREDIENTS

I can of refrigerated biscuits (I would use the jumbo size biscuits) pizza dough. Even refrigerated pie crusts can be substituted, ...10-4-$10 <$1

¼ c pizza or spaghetti sauce $1

1 c mozzarella cheese $1

1-6 oz package pepperoni, slice or dice.............................$1

½ c stir fry peppers & onions $1

1 jar marinated mushrooms, sliced $1

1 tbsp chopped garlic or ½ tsp garlic powder $1

½ c cottage cheese ....$1 or 10-4-$10

¼ c frozen spinach thawed/drained $1

DIRECTIONS

▶ Preheat oven to 375 degrees

▶ Roll pizza/biscuit dough into a 12" round

▶ Sauté the minced garlic, mushrooms, peppers, and onions in cooking oil until translucent

▶ S&P2T and then drain

▶ On the entire dough circle, spread a thin layer of sauce, leaving ½ inch edge

▶ Place all ingredients on ½ of dough, wet edge with water

▶ Fold opposite half over the half topped with sautéed vegetables, spinach, pepperoni, mushrooms and cheese

▶ Crimp edge with fork, being careful not to poke holes

▶ Place on a lightly greased cookie sheet or pizza sheet

▶ Bake in oven for approximately 25-30 minutes

▶ Let cool slightly so cheese won't slide out when cutting

▶ Pour pizza sauce over top of calzone

▶ Serve hot

$1Diva FYI

$ Serve hot and top with additional sauce.

$ Follow above recipe without the cottage cheese filling, and this will become a divalicious stromboli. Again, feel free to use canned (drained), frozen (thawed and drained), or fresh vegetables.

Oyster Stromboli

Speaking of stromboli, it appears that I've been treating the $1 Store's canned smoked oysters and clams like stepchildren. I only could find one use for the smoked oysters in my $1 Store Po' Boy Sandwich. Late one Friday night, I was watching an episode of "Rachel Ray On the Road". She and her husband were visiting the San Juan Islands in Washington state. Rachel's husband ordered an oyster stromboli. The camera panned in for a cross section view of the heavy oyster laden stromboli. You guessed it... the light bulb went off, and here was a perfect Dollar Diva recipe for the smoked oysters that I would see during each $1 Store visit. I made this oyster, mushroom and cheese-filled pastry for my Tuesday afternoon Bible Study participants. When I returned to church to pick up my serving dishes, all that was left from the stromboli was the platter I served it on and a piece of the crust.

INGREDIENTS

1 frozen pizza crust, thawed ....10-4-$10
1 can smoked oysters $1
2 4 oz can mushrooms ....<$1
1 3 oz bag mozzarella cheese $1
2 cloves garlic, chopped ....Pantry or $1
1 tbsp butter/margarine ....Pantry or <$1
Sprinkle of flour/cornmeal ....Pantry

DIRECTIONS:

▶ Drain oysters and mushrooms
▶ Preheat oven to 375 degrees
▶ Lightly grease pizza pan and sprinkle with flour and cornmeal
▶ Unroll thawed pie crust
▶ Place pie crust on pizza pan
▶ Sauté mushrooms in butter/margarine to reduce "fresh" taste (optional), drain well, then add chopped garlic

- ▶ On half of the pie crust layer ½ of mozzarella cheese, leaving ¾ edge for sealing stromboli
- ▶ Layer mushrooms and garlic on top of mozzarella cheese
- ▶ Layer oysters on top of mushrooms
- ▶ Layer remaining cheese on top of oyster layer
- ▶ SP2T
- ▶ Moisten ¾ edge with water
- ▶ Fold the other half of pie crust over the stromboli filling
- ▶ Either crimp with fork or pinch crust edges to seal stromboli

- ▶ Place stromoli in oven for 25-30 minutes
- ▶ Remove when crust is a nice light brown color
- ▶ Allow to cool slightly
- ▶ Garnish with either basil, parsley, oregano or some Italian season.

$Diva Tips

$ Add cup of spinach, or artichoke, or tomatoes etc. Depending on oven temperature, may have increase baking time slightly.

$ Follow above recipe with the cottage cheese filling, and this will become a divalicious calzone. Again, feel free to use canned (drained), frozen (thawed/drained) fresh vegetables.

Divalicious Menus with Ingredients Costing $1 or Less

Clam Chowder

When I moved back to the Philadelphia area, I spent a lot of time with my Grandmother, Cepha Thornton. For months, Marques and I would travel on SEPTA (public transportation) from Germantown to Bryn Mawr, no less than twice a week. I would go shopping for Grandmom, and found out that one of her favorite soups was clam chowder and oyster stew. I trust you'll find this rich and creamy New England Clam Chowder divalicious good and very easy to prepare.

INGREDIENTS

1 can whole white potatoes .... $1/<$1

1 stalk celery .... Pantry or Produce Market

1 small onion .... Pantry or Produce Market

1 can chopped clams $1

1 4 oz can mushrooms .... <$1

1 can evaporated milk OR
    1 container heavy cream .... Pantry or <$1

2 tbsp butter/margarine... Pantry

Croutons (optional) $1

DIRECTIONS:

▶ Set oven to 350 degrees

▶ Drain clams and mushrooms

▶ Drain potatoes and dice potatoes, celery and onions into bite size pieces

▶ Place large sauce pan on medium heat and melt butter/margarine, but don't allow it to brown (this is a light creamy colored soup)

- Saute mushrooms, onions & celery until translucent, then add potatoes
- Allow all vegetables to be covered with butter/margarine
- Sprinkle 3 tbsp of flour over vegetables; SP2T
- Stir gently until all vegetables are covered
- Slowly add evaporated milk
- Stew base will become a little thick (I add a little bit of nutmeg)
- Reduce heat to low and stir often
- Place clams in an oven-safe serving soup bowl
- Pour stew base into soup bowl
- Place clam chowder in oven and continue to cook in 350 degree oven for approx 15 to 20 minutes
- Remove and top with croutons, herbs, cheese etc, optional.

This is an absolutely diva-creamy-licious chowder!

Divalicious Menus with Ingredients Costing $1 or Less

Oyster Stew

This recipe's preparation process may appear to be lengthy, but it's truly worth it. This oyster stew is a really robust divalicious dish. This is good comfort food, too. Another of my Grandmother's favorites

INGREDIENTS

1 can whole white potatoes $1

1 stalk celery ....Pantry or Produce Market

1 small onion ....Pantry or Produce Market

1 can smoked oysters $1

1 4 oz can mushrooms ....<$1

1 can evaporated milk...<$1

1/2 cup frozen peas & carrots thawed and drained (optional)$1

2 tbsp butter/margarine..Pantry

3tbsp flour ....Pantry or $1

Croutons (optional) $1

Dining With the Dollar Diva

DIRECTIONS:

- Set oven to 350 degrees
- Drain oysters and mushrooms
- Drain potatoes and dice potatoes, celery and onions into bite size pieces
- Place large sauce pan on medium heat, melt butter/margarine and don't allow to brown (this is a light creamy colored soup)
- Saute mushrooms, onions & celery until translucent, then add potatoes
- Allow all vegetables to be covered with butter/margarine
- Sprinkle 3 tbsp of flour over vegetables, stir gently until all vegetables are covered
- Slowly add evaporated milk, stew base will become a little thick (I add a little bit of nutmeg)
- Reduce heat to low and stir often
- Place oysters in an oven-safe serving soup bowl with peas and carrots (peas &carrots are optional)
- Pour stew base into soup bowl
- Place oyster stew in oven and continue to cook at 350 degrees for approx 15 to 20 minutes
- Remove from oven and top with croutons; you can also add top with herbs (fresh/dried) and grated cheese as an option

Divalicious Menus with Ingredients Costing $1 or Less

Ms. Jeri's Meatball Ravioli Lasagna

When I first joined Bethel AME Bryn Mawr Church, I was blessed to become friends with Sis. Jeri Plange and her best friend, Sis. Marian Jones. Both Ms. Marian and Ms. Jeri grew up in Bethel Bryn Mawr, and both of them were on the Steward Board, long standing members of Bethel's Homecoming Committee, and they sang on the Senior Choir for many years. The two of them together or separately were real characters. Ms. Jeri wrote poetry, and she could tell a story that would make William Shakespeare look like an amateur. Back in the early 90's, Ms. Marian passed away. Being that I was Bethel's church secretary and had a mastery of WORDPERFECT® (remem-

ber that software?), Ms. Jeri paid me a visit at my home to work on the Sr. Choir's resolution for Ms. Marian's funeral. Remember I told you that Ms. Jeri could spin a yarn that would end up being a sweater, so what probably should have been a 30-45 minute meeting resulted in a four hour talk fest (Ms. Jeri doing the majority of the talking), and we ended up eating dinner, dessert and swapping recipes. Ms. Jeri ran this meatball stew recipe by me, and it didn't sound quite appealing, but being her junior, I agreed with her that it sounded delicious. Ms. Jeri passed away in December 2002, (I still keep her obituary in my Bible) and I truly miss our talks, disagreements, phone calls, emails, and laughing with one another. Every time I see a bag of meatballs at the $1 Store, her meatball stew recipe comes to mind. I thought that somehow, someway, I must pay homage to my beloved Ms. Jeri with a recipe with meatballs. This divalicious meatball ravioli recipe came to mind. Seyena, Chucky, Megan, and Lindsi, this recipe is in honor of your mother and grandmother and my good friend, Ms. Jeri.

Dining With the Dollar Diva

INGREDIENTS

1 bag of meatballs, thawed $1
1 roll hot/mild sausage $1
1 jar/can of spaghetti sauce $1
1-2 oz can of tomato paste (optional I like my sauce thick) <$1
1 can diced tomatoes ....<$1
1 jar 16 oz marinated mushrooms, sliced $1
1 bag of stir fry peppers and onions $1
3 tbsp minced garlic...$1
½ bag of chopped spinach, thawed/drained.......................$1
16 oz of cottage cheese (drained)......................................$1
2 c shredded mozzarella cheese ....$1 or 10-4-$10
1c shredded cheddar cheese ....$1 or 10-4-$10
2 bags of ravioli –thawed $1
Dried herbs~basil, parsley, Italian seasonings, oregano, ...
....$1/Fresh
2 tbsp oil (depending upon the fat in the sausage) ....Pantry
2tbsp sugar-optional (I like my sauce sweet, I may use more)..
....Pantry or <$1

DIRECTIONS

▶ Preheat oven to 350 degrees
▶ In a preheated deep skillet, add oil, and then brown meatballs, sausage
▶ Sauté mushrooms, onions and peppers, S&P2T, drain
▶ Stir in ½ of the chopped garlic
▶ If using tomato paste, make a hot spot in center of pan and add tomato paste in that spot. This will take away the "fresh" tomato paste taste
▶ Add spaghetti sauce and tomatoes, S&P2T
▶ Add a dash of sugar (brown sugar gives sauce a richer taste)
▶ Add dried herbs (if using fresh add to the cheese mixture)
▶ Simmer on low heat for 20 minutes

Divalicious Menus with Ingredients Costing $1 or Less

▶ In a separate bowl, mix cottage cheese, ½ shredded mozzarella, all cheddar, and spinach

▶ S&P2T

▶ In a lightly greased baking dish, put a spoonful of sauce in bottom of dish.

▶ Start the layering process layer ravioli, layer cheese mixture, layer sauce, the last layer should be topped with the remaining shredded cheese.

▶ Place in over for 30-40 minutes covered

▶ Bake uncovered for the remaining 15-20 minutes.

▶ Set for about 10 minutes before cutting. However, if you like, refrigerate after cooling, and reheat the next day. Absolutely heaven!!! Top with remaining sauce if you have any left.

$1 Diva FYI

$ You may think that a lot of salt is used for this recipe, but use salt sparing each time you add additional ingredients to give it a "level of complexity", as Lydia on PBS says.

$ This may not be the best picture for this dish, but trust me it is absolutely divalicious!!!!

Seafood Jambalaya

Carol, a friend of mine, made this serious jambalya for one of her and husband's annual theme summer cookouts. It was absolutely beautiful, but, alas, she used a pork smoked sausage so I wasn't able to taste it, but remember, the eating process involves utilizing several of your five basic senses. First, there is the eye appealing visual. Then, you take pleasure in the aroma. Then you savor each bite. In this case, two outta three wasn't bad. Every now and then, you may be able to get smoked sausage kielbasa at the $1 Store, or the big box stores may have a special 10-4-$10 sale. When you see it, definitely stock up and FREEZE it!!! But you can use the regular roll sausage from the $1 Store.

INGREDIENTS

1 can of crushed tomatoes	$1
1-2 oz can of tomato paste-optional (I like my sauce thick)	<$1
1 can broth	<$1
1 bag of rice	$1
2 bouillon cubes	Pantry or <$1
1 bag frozen stir fry peppers & onions	$1
2-4 oz, cans mushrooms, sliced	<$1
½ jar chopped garlic	Pantry or <$1
1-5 oz bag shrimp	$1 or 10-4-$10
1-4 oz bag scallops	$1 or 10-4-$10
1 bag tilapia	$1 or 10-4-$10
1 bag salmon	$1 or 10-4-$10
1 bag flounder	$1 or 10-4-$10
1 pack smoked sausage, cut crosswise preferred	10-4-$10
1 tbsp balsamic vinegar	Pantry or $1
1 tbsp worcestershire sauce	Pantry or $1
1 tsp sage	Pantry or $1
1 tsp cayenne pepper	Pantry or $1
1/2 tsp cumin	Pantry or $1

Divalicious Menus with Ingredients Costing $1 or Less

1 tsp red pepper flakes ....Pantry or $1

DIRECTIONS

▶ Cook rice according to directions printed on package or use rice cooker, but use broth and bouillon cubes instead of water for a more flavorful rice

▶ In a preheated large skillet, add oil

▶ Brown tilapia, salmon and flounder

▶ Then add shrimp, and scallops, and cook until edges are pink

▶ S&P2T

▶ Remove from skillet

▶ Saute in same skillet stir fry onions & peppers, garlic, mushrooms, and brown both sausages,

▶ S&P2T, then drain, reserving approx 2 tbsp of grease,

▶ Make a "hole" in center of pan, pour in tomato paste and crushed tomatoes, and stir briskly

▶ Stir and incorporate all of the ingredients in the pan

▶ S&P2T, all seasonings/spices

▶ Fold rice into pan, and then fold all of the seafood back into the pan

▶ Place in oven at low heat uncovered for 10 minutes

▶ Remove from oven

▶ Let set for 2-3 minutes

▶ Serve hot

Tilapia Rollups

I worked with a guy who always had these mini-lasagna rollups for lunch. I couldn't imagine how my on-the-go bachelor co-worker was able to fix this multi-step pasta dish on a weeknight for lunch the next day. Then he told me that he just puts the lasagna noodles in hot water. He didn't boil them and he uses a jar meat sauce. He said this method reduces his prep time and makes a serious impression on his female dining companions. I modified his technique and instead rolled up the lasagna noodle with the cheese, a veggie and a fish fillet, so it would have all of the food groups. Isn't this a beautiful presentation??? Soooo... divalicious!!!! Here we go...

INGREDIENTS

6 lasagna noodles..$1

4 tilapia filets – thawed and halved $1

Divalicious Menus with Ingredients Costing $1 or Less

1-16 oz cottage cheese (small curd) drained.......................$1

1-½ bag of frozen broccoli-thawed & drained $1

1-3 oz bag of scallops (optional) $1

1-3 oz bag of shrimp (optional).......................................$1

2 tbsp chopped garlic or garlic powder $1

1 small onion – diced

½ cup diced roasted/marinated peppers
   (good color if you are using an alfredo sauce)..................$1

2 c mozzarella cheese ....$1 or 10-4-$10

¼ tsp each: nutmeg, oregano, and basil (can use fresh herbs)

1-28 oz jar of your favorite pasta sauce (red or white)

DIRECTIONS

▶ Preheat oven to 350 degrees

▶ Fill a baking dish with extremely hot salted water

▶ Lay lasagna noodles in baking dish and make sure noodles are completely covered with the extremely hot water

▶ Season thawed tilapia filets on both sides

▶ Cut in half lengthwise

▶ In a medium bowl, use hand mixer, and mix cottage cheese, ½ of mozzarella cheese, garlic, onions and seasonings, and S&P2T

▶ Fold in broccoli and other seafood if using. (Make sure broccoli is thawed and drained well. If not this will impact texture of filling and/or baking time)

▶ Lightly grease baking dish and put a ½ cup of pasta sauce in bottom of the baking dish

▶ Remove al dente lasagna noodles from water. They should be able to roll without breaking or tearing

- Top lasagna noodle with the two tilapia halves and cheese mixture
- Leave a 1" edge at end of the lasagne noodle, do not over stuff. Roll lasagna noodle tightly. May secure lasagna noodle with toothpick.
- Place in baking dish with edge side down
- Repeat this process until all rollups are done
- Pour sauce over rollups
- Reserve ½ cup of sauce
- Bake covered for 20 minutes
- Lower heat to 300 degrees
- Remove cover and sprinkle remaining cheese over top of rollups
- Bake an additional 5 minutes uncovered
- Remove from oven
- Let sit for 5 minutes
- Serve with additional sauce

$1 Diva FYI

$ Serve with garlic toast (Recipe should be somewhere in this book!)

Divalicious Menus with Ingredients Costing $1 or Less

Horn & Hardart at the $1 Store

Back in the day, when Donald and Lillian, my father and mother were still a couple, the seven of us, Daddy, Mommy and the Fisher Five used to go on fabulous vacations and outings to Canada, Atlantic City, Pittsburgh, Cincinnati, Baltimore, Washington, DC, and also way up to North Philly to see Daddy's Aunt Suzie and Uncle George, and even to his cousin Moses' farm in southern New Jersey. Cousin Moses raised corn and pigs and had an outhouse. Oh, the pig pen and outhouse stenches would hit us as soon as we were told we were going for a visit to Moses' house. But Cousin Moses' wife, Christine would serve us some of the best food ever. Wherever we traveled, no matter what interstate, turnpike, main highway, or back road we were on, before we arrived at home, we would wait for Daddy's famous line "Anybody wants ......eerts?" Right then and there, the Fisher Five would squeal with delight because we knew we were going to be going to either Howard Johnson's if this was a turnpike trip or Horn & Hardart Automat, 52nd & Market, or 63rd & Market in West Philly. Even though Mommy

Ðining With the Ðollar Ðiva

would act like she wanted to go straight home, you could bet the farm that she was already deciding what she was going to order. The funny thing was, we were only supposed to get dessert. But I would say 93.5% of the time, the entire family would end up getting a full meal, while Donald Fisher would get a cup of coffee and a slice of coconut custard pie. I always remembered that Daddy would drink a cold glass of water with every meal; he drank water long before it became in vogue, and he definitely wouldn't be a "fan" of today's bottled water. Tap water would be just fine for him. So, short story long, we would pull up in front of Horn and Hardart, or H&H as we called it, pile out of the car, and walk quickly across the street to get into the restaurant because we were afraid that they would close the doors right in front of us. As soon as we entered the Automat, we would hear the hustle and bustle of the customers, smell the rich aroma of the coffee, and then we would make a mad dash to get in line to select our meal with the cafeteria servers. Now, remember, we were only there for dessert, so after ordering our dinner from the automated servers, we'd move our trays down the line, and we were faced with a gargantuan, wall-sized self-service vending machine containing the best desserts you could find anywhere!!! We'd turn to Daddy to get our quarters, dimes and nickels so we could drop the correct amount into the multi-compartments and retrieve our "....eerts" of choice. My H & H favorite was Salisbury steak w/gravy, macaroni with stewed tomatoes, the best creamed spinach in the world, a tea biscuit with butter, and apple dumpling with warm custard sauce (it didn't photograph well). I can still visualize my tray and taste that memorable meal that I ordered so many times. This was the ultimate fast food.

Gas and tolls for roundtrip visit to relatives in Turnersville, NJ—probably less than $7.00.

Dinner and 'eerrts for a family of seven at H & H—probably about $15.00.

Childhood memories of vacations with my father, mother and the Fisher Five—priceless! Those times in my life were unforgettable. I hope that these inexpensive recipes do H & H and Daddy proud.

Divalicious Menus with Ingredients Costing $1 or Less

Salisbury Steak

INGREDIENTS

1 roll of ground turkey $1

1 roll sausage $1

½ bag stir fry onions & peppers $1

2 oz can mushrooms...<$1

2 tbsp minced garlic ....Pantry or $1

2 tsp Worcestershire sauce ....Pantry or $1

2 tsp balsamic vinegar ....Pantry or $1

1 c bread crumbs ....Pantry or $1

1 egg ....Pantry or $1

1 packet onion soup mix....................................Pantry or $1

1 jar brown gravy/or dry gravy mix ....Pantry or $1

DIRECTIONS

▶ Preheat large deep skillet on medium heat. Add cooking oil in pan

▶ Saute stir fry onions and peppers and mushrooms until caramelized

▶ Remove from pan

▶ Mix ground turkey and sausage, onion soup, egg, breadcrumb, and minced garlic together, until incorporated

▶ Shape into mini meatloafs

▶ Place Salisbury steaks in pan; don't overcrowd

▶ Cook 3 minutes on each side. Remove from pan

▶ Pour gravy into pan, or if using a powdered gravy mix, make according to package directions

▶ Season with Worcestershire sauce, S&P2T

▶ Place Salisbury steaks and caramelized onions, peppers and mushrooms back into pan

▶ Cover and simmer at medium low heat for 10 minutes

▶ Remove from heat, uncover and let rest for 5 minutes

▶ Serve hot

Divalicious Menus with Ingredients Costing $1 or Less

Creamed Spinach

INGREDIENTS

1-16 oz bag frozen spinach $1

1 can evaporated milk ....<$1

  OR 1 heavy cream $1

3 tsp cornstarch or flour..Pantry

3 tbsp butter ....Pantry

¼ cup onions (diced) ....Pantry or Produce Market

Pinch of nutmeg $1

Pinch of sugar $1

DIRECTIONS

▶ Melt butter in a medium size sauce pan

▶ Lightly saute onions

▶ Stir in cornstarch/flour

▶ Pour in evaporated milk or heavy cream to make a roux

▶ Whisk constantly to remove all lumps

▶ Fold in spinach (if not thawed, make allowances for amount of liquid)

▶ S&P2T

▶ Add nutmeg and sugar

▶ Bring to slow boil, stir constantly to prevent scorching

▶ Cover and reduce to a low heat,

▶ Simmer at low temp for 15 minutes

$DIVA FYI

$ If your creamed spinached is too thick, stir in additional milk/cream until you get your desired consistency.

Macaroni & Cheese

INGREDIENTS

1-8 oz containers white or yellow cheddar cheese spread/dip.....$1

1 c Monterey Jack cheese ....10-4-$10

1 c cheddar cheese ....10-4-$10

1 box rigatoni..$1

2 tbsp butter/margarine....................................Pantry or <$1

2 tsp flour/cornstarch ....Pantry or <$1

8 oz diced tomatoes (drained WELL)..................................$1

1-6 oz can evaporated milk...............................Pantry or <$1

DIRECTIONS

▶ Preheat oven to 325 degrees

▶ Generously grease baking dish

▶ Cook pasta according to package directions

▶ Drain and return pasta to pan

▶ Fold in butter, S&P2T

▶ Place saucepan containing evaporated milk and cheese spread over medium-low heat

▶ Add cheddar and Monterey Jack cheese

▶ Stir constantly to prevent scorching

▶ Allow cheese to melt slowly

▶ Fold in drained tomatoes

▶ S&P2T

▶ Lower heat

▶ Pour pasta into cheese sauce, stir well so all pasta is covered with cheese sauce

▶ Pour into lightly greased baking dish and place in oven

▶ Bake for 15 minute

▶ Remove from oven

▶ Set for 5 minutes before serving

Divalicious Menus with Ingredients Costing $1 or Less

Tea Biscuits

INGREDIENTS

1 package biscuit mix $1

¾ c milk ....Pantry or $1

4 eggs ....Pantry or $1

½ c sugar ....Pantry or $1

1 tsp vanilla ....Pantry or $1

1 cup raisins ....Pantry or $1

½ tsp baking powder ....Pantry or $1

3 tbsp butter ....Pantry or $1

DIRECTIONS

▶ Preheat oven 325 degrees

▶ Combine biscuit mix, baking powder and raisins together

▶ In separate bowl mix three eggs, milk, sugar, and vanilla together

▶ Combine wet and dry ingredients, do not over mix

▶ Roll out dough on floured surface and knead (do not over knead)

▶ Cut out biscuits using biscuit cutter

▶ Place on greased baking sheet

▶ Prepare egg wash with remaining egg and a couple of tsp of water/milk and brush on top of each biscuit

▶ Bake according to package directions

▶ Remove from oven, and coat biscuit tops with butter

▶ Let cool slightly, serve with butter and jam

Apple Dumpling With Warm Custard Sauce

INGREDIENTS

1 jar apples -drained $1

1 pie crust (I use Jiffy for this recipe)....................Pantry or $1

1 tsp butter/margerine.......................................Pantry or $1

1 tsp vanilla ....Pantry or $1

1 c sugar ....Pantry or $1

1/2 c cinnamon & nutmeg...................................Pantry or $1

1 tsp lemon juice ....Pantry or $1

Pinch of salt ....Pantry or $1

4 snak pack vanilla pudding
  OR or 1 box of instant pudding mix ....Pantry or $1

DIRECTIONS

▶ Preheat oven to 375 degrees

▶ Use 1/2 of pie crust mix (or make the entire box and refrigerate what you don't use)

▶ Split pie crust into two halves

▶ In bowl mix apples, vanilla, sugar, cinnamon & nutmeg and lemon juice

▶ Place apple filling in center of pie crusts

▶ Break up butter into pieces

▶ Place on top of apple filling

▶ Overlap pie crust over filling, take fork poke few holes on top

▶ Place on lightly greased baking sheet

▶ Bake for 25 and minutes, remove from oven

▶ Microwave pudding in a separate bowl until warm

▶ Or if using instant pudding prepare according to package directions and warm in microwave

▶ Pour over dumpling

▶ Serve hot

Divalicious Menus with Ingredients Costing $1 or Less

$1 Diva FYI:

$ Can use refrigerated pie crust, but I just prefer the texture of the boxed pie crust for this recipe.

$ Use any canned or jarred fruit, and make sure to drain well.

Mock "Lobster" Pie

Years ago at a Sterling Club meeting, Aunti Barbara made this truly exquisite Lobster Pie. One of our members called this culinary work of art a casserole, and I immediately ducked, because Aunti shot our member a look that would kill a rhinocerous at 25 paces. First, neither Aunti or I are fans of imitation crab, but this was a reliable ingredient since monk fish is no longer an inexpensive fish. So, with much trial and error and using the imitation seafood, lobster or crab and the various shrimp, scallops, tilapia, flounder, etc. that's sold either 10-4-$10 or at the $1 Store, I was able to come up with a viable substitute lobster pie. Aunti Babs, this reproduction mock lobster pie is in no way a disrespect to your luscious lobster pie. But you know what they say, imitation is the best form of flattery.

Divalicious Menus with Ingredients Costing $1 or Less

INGREDIENTS

1 prepared pie crust, or rolled pie crust or 1 can refrigerated biscuits ....10-4-$10

1 package imitation seafood, lobster or crab ....10-4-$10

1-3 oz bags shrimp (peeled) $1

1-3 oz scallops $1

1-3 oz bag flounder $1

1-3 oz bag tilapia $1

1 can cream of celery soup...<$1

1 jar/can mushrooms –sliced/drained ....<$1

½ can evaporated milk or heavy cream ....Pantry or $1

½ tbsp flour or cornstarch ....Pantry or $1

2 tbsp butter ....Pantry or $1

1/8 cup roasted peppers $1

3 tbsp diced onions

S2YT dill (dried or fresh) ....Pantry or $1

S2YT parsley (dried or fresh) ....Pantry or $1

DIRECTIONS

▶ Preheat oven to 325 degrees

▶ Prepare pie crust or biscuit dough that you are using

▶ Heat large sauce pot at medium temp

▶ Melt 1 tbsp butter to sauté mushrooms and onions

▶ Add flour/cornstarch to make a roux

▶ Stir in milk, and let thicken

▶ Whisk in soup, make sure there are no lumps

▶ Add roasted peppers (for color)

▶ Lightly dust all seafood

▶ In separate skillet use remaining butter and brown seafood (don't overcrowd)

▶ Fold seafood ingredients into thickened soup mixture

▶ Sprinkle in dill and parsley, and SP2T to taste

▶ Fill pie crust with seafood mixture

▶ Bake for approximately 35 minutes; pie crust is brown and firm

▶ Remove from oven, let cool for about 5 minutes then serve

$1Diva FYI

$ If using a rolled pie crust or biscuit dough, for a prettier presentation, use a smaller baking dish so surplus dough can be folded over top of the pie.

$ For this recipe fresh herbs are preferred but feel free to use dried herbs.

Divalicious Menus with Ingredients Costing $1 or Less

Peas and Carrot Bisque

I made this soup without writing down the recipe, or I didn't save it properly. Have to stop doing that, huh? Anyway, on the way home from visiting my stepson, Harold, in Tampa, Florida, Marques and I stopped off at one of the more popular southern family chain restaurants for dinner. I've been to a few of these chain restaurants, but this one really wasn't a good representation of the service and good wholesome food that I'm accustomed to. But that's another story for another time. As my son Marques' order was overloaded with starchy carb sides, I told him to get a green vegetable. To my surprise, he ordered carrots. I looked at him, like "Yeah, right. You're gonna eat carrots." And that's when Marques told me that he loves carrots. Then I racked my brain for a recipe where the main ingredient was carrots. So, I got the brilliant idea of a creamed carrot bisque with peas. Now this may not sound appetizing, but look at the picture. It's an absolutely beautiful dish and is quite delicious. Try using cream of coconut milk or heavy cream instead of evaporated or regular milk for extra richness. Can anyone say "divalicious"?

This may not be your shot but, my child, who is not a soup eater, really enjoyed this bisque.

INGREDIENTS

1 can (drained) or ½ bag frozen carrots (thawed, sliced, whole) $1

½ can vegetable broth (okay to use chicken) $1

1 large potato or ½ can of potatoes ....Pantry or $1

3 tbsp butter/margarine....................................Pantry or $1

2 tbsp flour ....Pantry

1 can evaporated/cream of coconut milk ....Pantry or $1

1 cup peas (preferably frozen)...$1

¼ tsp nutmeg, cinnamon....................................Pantry or $1

SP2T

DIRECTIONS

▶ Melt 2 tbsp butter/margarine in a medium-size suacepan

▶ Stir in flour

▶ Pour chicken/vegetable broth to make roux

▶ When mixture thickens, turn down heat

▶ Add carrots, the potato and spices, allow vegetables to get warm.

▶ Pour entire contents into blender/food processor

▶ Pulse several times until all ingredients are well blended, mixture is still thick

▶ Make sure you leave room at the top of the blender because warm food will expand and while blender is pulsing food it may overflow.

▶ Pour soup from blender back into saucepan

▶ Put on medium-low heat

▶ Stir in milk until soup reaches desired consistency

▶ Add remaining butter/margarine, stir, and let simmer for 10 minutes

▶ Stir in frozen peas

▶ Cover until peas are cooked but still a bright green color

▶ Serve immediately.

$1 Diva FYI

$ Top with sour cream, croutons and sprinkle with parsley, or use other garnishes from your refrigerator or cupboard.

$ Cumin is an excellent spice to use with this soup, but a little does go a long way. So, if you use it, use sparingly.

Divalicious Menus with Ingredients Costing $1 or Less

Fish Fried Rice

Years ago, my nephew Ricky introduced me to this really tasty fish fried rice dish from a Muslim carry out in Mt. Airy. Not only was the fried rice delicious, but this dish had the biggest pieces of the most mouth watering fried whiting you could find. Unfortunately, the three Philadelphia locations that I know of have closed their doors. Below is a $1Store replica of that really satisfying Asian cusine.

INGREDIENTS

1-16 oz package of rice (brown rice is excellent) $1

1 bag tilapia $1

1 bag flounder $1

1 c vegetable oil ....Pantry or $1

½ cup flour ....Pantry or $1

½ cup breadcrumbs...Pantry or $1

½ bag 16 oz bag stir fry onions & peppers (thawed/drained) $1

1 c frozen mix vegetables (thawed and drained) $1

½ c frozen broccoli thawed (drained) $1

Hot peppers of your choice $1

4 oz can sliced mushrooms ....<$1

S2YT Soy sauce $1

S&P2T

DIRECTIONS

▶ Cook rice according to package directions

▶ Preheat skillet on medium high

▶ Add oil, reserve 2 tbsp to caramelize vegetables

▶ Flour/dredge all fish

▶ Fry, S&P2T and drain

▶ In separate sauce pan heat 2 tbsp vegetable oil on medium high heat, stir fry onions and peppers, mushrooms, broccoli, and mixed vegetables

▶ Add cooked rice and season with soy sauce

▶ Cut up fish filets into quarter pieces and add to rice

▶ Serve hot

$DIVA FYI

$ Use broth or stock instead of water when cooking rice. Definitely gives it more flavor.

Divalicious Menus with Ingredients Costing $1 or Less

Juliet's Chicken

The entire time this book was being edited by Juliet, the proofreade,r and Sheilah, my pubisher, in the The Elevator Group office, they both kept badgering me that I had to be consistent in putting the measurement amounts for each and every recipe. Juliet consistently harped that she wasn't a cook so the measurements were an absolute must. I just rolled my eyes in the back of my head and said "Whatever!!!!" Then I said you know I have told them that I had the easiest, divalicious baked chicken recipe that even Juliet, the non-cook, could make. And I told them, Juliet told me to stop giving out free recipes. Almost simultaneously, Juliet and Sheilah ordered me to put the recipe in the book! So here it is...

INGREDIENTS

1 lb chicken breast or thighs ....10-4,-$10
¼ c oil or butter/margarine $1
S&P2T
Balsamic vinegar (optional)..$1

DIRECTIONS

▶ Preheat oven to 500 degrees
▶ Coat chicken with oil of choice. If using butter or margarine, melt then pour/baste over chicken breasts or thighs
▶ Season well with salt and pepper
▶ Add a splash of balsamic vinegar (again this is optional)
▶ Place on light greased baking sheet
▶ Bake for approximately 10 minutes; skin will get good and crispy
▶ Turn heat down to 325 degrees, cook until juices run clear, approximately 25 minutes
▶ Remove from heat
▶ Set for 5 minutes then serve

Mc$1 Store Eggs Benedict

This is an upscale, economical, divalicious Eggs Benedict recipe and all of the ingredients can be purchased at the $1 Store.

INGREDIENTS

2 English muffins $1

½ roll loose sausage roll $1

4 eggs $1

SP2T and pinch of nutmeg ....Pantry

½ cup frozen spinach thawed and drained..........................$1

¼ c milk or heavy cream ....Pantry or $1

½ cup Cheese dip (light colored) $1

¼ cup Cheddar cheese $1

1 tbsp margarine ....Pantry

DIRECTIONS

▶ Preheated oven to 350 degrees to brown English muffins or use toaster, butter each toasted half

▶ Microwave spinach drain and set aside

▶ Preheat lightly greased skillet on medium heat

▶ Make 4 thin sausage patties, the size of the English muffins and fry in skillet until done, then remove from skillet

▶ Preheat clean skillet on medium heat, melt shortening (do not allow to brown), reduce heat to low

▶ Beat the eggs, add splash of milk, S&P2T

▶ Pour scrambled eggs into skillet, stir constantly, remove from heat eggs are at your desired texture

▶ Microwave cheese dip to a smooth creamy consistency, add milk or heavy cream

▶ Stir in cheddar cheese until completely melted, may need to microwave for a few seconds

▶ Top each English muffin half with the cooked drained spinach

▶ Top spinach with the sausage patties

▶ Top sausage patties with the scrambled eggs

▶ Pour melted cheese sauce over the eggs

▶ Garnish with parsley, or dill (or dried/fresh herb of choice) and paprika

$DIVA FYI:

$ Substitute poached or fried eggs for scrambled eggs.

$ Substitute sausage with either tilapia, salmon or flounder filets.

Divalicious Menus with Ingredients Costing $1 or Less

Notes

Dining With the Dollar Diva

Notes

Divalicious Menus with Ingredients Costing $1 or Less

Notes

Dining With the Dollar Diva

Divalicious Menus with Ingredients Costing $1 or Less

Sweets, Desserts, & Pastries For Your Sweet Tooth

Sweets, Desserts & Pastries For Your Sweet tooth

$Diva Tips

$ Using your drinking glasses for your biscuit cutter? Tired of ending up with monstrous size biscuits? Remove both lids from a soup, tomato paste, or vegetable can, wash, and let dry thoroughly. Perfect size biscuits every time. Before cutting biscuits, dip rim of can in flour so it won't stick to dough.

$ Remember to purchase those squeeze limes and lemons from the $1 Store. A couple of squirts on your fruits will keep them from turning brown. Also use in pie fillings.

$ Don't walk away when your desserts are under the broiler. Sugar will burn extremely fast.

$ Check out your drugstores/pharmacies for seasonings, spices, and extracts, they are famous for having weekly two for $1 sales.

$ Many of the canned fruits used in these recipes were purchased at the $1Store, but check out the big box stores or the small discount stores you may be able to get the fruits for less than $1.

$ Dried fruits and nuts can be purchased for $1 or less at your local drugstores/pharmacies.

$ When baking try using applesauce or pureed baby food fruit instead of oil, butter, or margarine in your recipes.

Vanilla Napoleon Rounds

Back in the day when I lived in DC, I used to ride my bike to work, not for solely for health reasons, or conserve gas, but because it gave me an

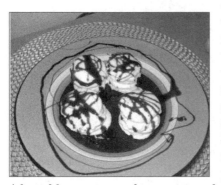

opportunity to ride by some of the most historic sites in our nation's capitol and mingle with the residents and businesses of the diverse cultures and neighbors. Plus, I knew I looked good riding around town on my metallic red Motobécane® bicycle that Marques' father gave me for my 22nd birthday. Every payday, I would ride through the Adams Morgan area and pay a visit to the local caterer whose bakery was open to the public. I would treat myself to two of the world's most decadent éclairs. The lightly sweetened flaky pastry shell was a perfect compliment to the thick and rich custard pudding that was inside. A sensual layer of dark chocolate was piped on top. That was the one day that my boss Loretta knew I would be on time, because I would sit in the back of the data entry office and just eat myself silly. And oh yeah, there were sound effects too, smacking my lips, oh man this is good, aaaaaaaaaahhhhh. I think that I was even eating with my mouth open. Anyway…one day, the bakery didn't have my éclairs, and I was simply pissed. So the pastry chef came to the counter and said "Try my napoleons, they are quite good." I was like, "NO" he said, I'll give you a half dozen for free" I said "Wrap them up" Needless to say, my following visit I asked for one napoleon and one éclair, and the pastry chef always made sure that the bakery had them ready for me too. I know that this recipe is not the mouthwatering French pastry that I long for, but hopefully you will find it to be a satisfying substitute.

INGREDIENTS

1 pkg refrigerated rolled pie crusts, thawed at room
  temperature ....10-4-$10

½ c confectioner's sugar ....Pantry or $1

1-8 oz cream cheese ....$1 or <$1

1 box instant vanilla pudding ....<$1 (or use 2 snak cups)

1 can vanilla/buttercream frosting $1

2 tbsp chocolate sauce ....Pantry or $1

1 tsp vanilla ....Pantry or $1

3 tbsp milk ....Pantry or $1

DIRECTIONS

▶ Preheat oven according to directions printed on pie crusts package

▶ In a medium size bowl, using hand mixer, whip cream cheese and confectioner's sugar together, then mix in pudding at a med-high speed until mixture is smooth and thick

▶ Unroll pie crusts on lighty-floured surface

▶ Cut into circles using a 2" round cookie/biscuit cutter

▶ Sprinkle with sugar

▶ Place on lightly greased baking sheet

▶ Bake according to package directions, and remove when crusts are baked and have a flaky texture

▶ Chill pudding mixture until firm

▶ In another bowl, dilute frosting with milk (use sparingly until you get the desired consistency/smoothness)

▶ Place two melon scoops of filling on 2/3 of napoleons rounds (1 each napoleon will require 3 pastry rounds)

▶ Place 1 filling topped pastry round on top of another filling topped pastry round and top it with a plain pastry round. (Each napoleon will have two layers of filling and 3 pastry rounds)

▶ When all the layering is completed; pour frosting over the top rounds and let set

▶ Squeeze chocolate sauce into a tablespoon, then hold spoon over napoleon, and lightly drizzle napoleons with chocolate sauce

Fruit Tart

This fruit tart just got more interesting and prettier. For years, the $1 Store has sold 12 oz bags of frozen strawberries, but recently they've had 16 oz bags of frozen mixed berries and 12 oz bags of blueberries. If you get them at your local $1 Store, I would strongly recommend that you stock up as they may not have them in the future. The same goes for pie crust, but then again there's always the ever reliable refrigerated crescent dough.

INGREDIENTS
1 package rolled pie crust, or crescent refrigerated dough
1 can sliced peaches (drained) ....<$1
1 can sliced pears (drained) ....<$1
1 can crushed pineapples (drained ....<$1
1-16 oz bag of frozen mix fruit (drained) $1
1 c sugar ....Pantry or $1
1 tsp vanilla, cinnamon, and nutmeg, to taste.....................$1
½ tsp lemon juice $1
2 tbsp cornstarch or flour....................................Pantry or $1
½ c butter or margarine.......................................Pantry or $1
1 beaten egg for egg wash-optional ....Pantry or $1

DIRECTIONS
▶ Preheat oven 325 degrees
▶ Drain peaches, pears, and crushed pineapples (reserve juice for syrup for ice tea!!)
▶ Let pie crusts come to room temperature for easy unrolling
▶ Roll out crusts into pie pan or tart baking dish
▶ After fruits have drained thoroughly, fold together carefully not to break up fruit (especially the berries)
▶ Add sugar, vanilla, spices, salt lemon juice and cornstarch/flour
▶ Make sure dried ingredients are mixed well (no noticeable lumps)

Divalicious Menus with Ingredients Costing $1 or Less

▶ Pour fruit filling in center of pie crust leaving a 2 inch edge

▶ Turn up 2 inch edge of crust over the fruit filling

▶ Crimp if desired

▶ Slice butter/margarine and place over fruit

▶ Wet edge with water (or egg wash) as crust will brown before the tart has finished baking

▶ Bake for 35-45 minutes depending on your oven

▶ Serve hot, warm, or cold. Top with ice cream or whipped toping it will be divalicious no matter what!!!!

$1 Diva FYI:

$ If you don't have all of the listed fruits available, you can still make this tart/pie. I've used this for recipe for a blueberry peach tart and it is absolutely divadarngood!!!!

Elder Denise's Lemon Berry Parfait

For years I've made numerous variations of that famous Cool Whip® yogurt pie recipe, but the only person who really enjoyed it besides me was Bethel's former assistant pastor, Rev. Denise Reynolds. Well, over two years ago Rev. Denise, became the lead Elder of her own church Mt. Joy Church of God. So now I really don't have anyone to help eat this pie, so I kinda stopped making it it. Then I saw these really basic but elegant goblets at the $1 Store and I said to myself, hmmmm.. that would be an excellent way to serve an individual portion. Especially since the $1 Store now sells 16 oz bags of mixed berries, this makes such a beautiful presentation. This is a take-off on my yogurt pie recipe. You can make the filling and pour it the into a glass goblet layered with crushed graham crackers or cookies and berries, then chill until firm. Serving in this in a beautiful goblet for a single serving for that special someone, YOU!!!

INGREDIENTS

1 package instant lemon pudding mix ....<$1

1 8 oz cream cheese ....$1 or <$1

1 can lemon pie filling $1

1-16 oz tub of whipped topping ....<$1

1-16 oz bag of frozen fruit (strawberries are a $1 store staple, but recently I found bags of mixed berries and blueberries. I stocked up on them as they may not have them regularly in future) $1

1 c crushed graham crackers or vanilla wafers or animal crackers (actually any cookie of your choice will work). Lemon sandwich cookies is a nice touch as Lydia B from PBS says "another level of complexity" $1

1 cup sugar ....Pantry or $1

1 tsp lemon extract...Pantry or $1

1 tsp vanilla ....Pantry or $1

1 can of dairy/non-dairy whipped topping.........................$1

DIRECTIONS:

- Macerate/thaw berries with ½ cup of sugar to give a rich flavor add a dash of vanilla extract
- Crush cookies in a 1 quart size freezer bag
- Using a hand mixer in a medium mixing bowl, mix together the instant pudding mix, cream cheese, vanilla and the sugar until smooth.
- Fold in the can of lemon pie filling
- Fold in the entire 16 oz containerwhipped topping
- Chill in refrigerator until parfait is firm and ready to serve
- Mix lemon pudding according to directions on box, fold entire can of lemon pie filling
- Serve in wine goblets
- Place layer of the crushed cookies, layer of the parfait, and a layer of the berries
- Repeat until goblet is filled
- Top with the dairy whipped topping and a few berries
- Depending upon the consistency of the parfait will determine how long you should take before serving to your guests. or return to refrigerator until ready to serve.

Divalicious Menus with Ingredients Costing $1 or Less

Ice Cream Cake

Have you ever seen that really annoying commercial from the nationally known ice cream manufacturer about the ice cream cake where the dinosaur, Lego® figures, the spaceman, soccer player and the cheerleaders etc. are jumping up and down. Maybe not as annoying as my stories, huh???? Well now it's not so irritating because I was able to get an inexpensive ice cream cake recipe for my troubles at the $1 Store.

INGREDIENTS

1 yellow pound cake $1

1 quart of ice cream – softened $1

1-16oz bag frozen fruit (optional) $1

2 containers of frosting $1

1 tsp orange extract ....Pantry or $1

1/2 c sugar ....Pantry or $1

DIRECTIONS:

▶ Macerate/thaw berries with ½ cup of sugar to give a rich flavor

▶ Add a dash of orange extract

▶ Slice cake in half lengthwise

▶ Place the top rounded upper half of cake cut side down on wax paper surface along side bottom half of cake

▶ Layer bottom half with softened ice cream, and layer berries over ice cream layer. Sprinkle layer of berries over ice cream

▶ Spread ice cream and berries even to ends of cake layer because you don't want the ice cream to spill out and make it difficult to frost the cake

▶ Place the top half of one cake over the bottom half of the other, cut side up (you may have to cut off rounded top of cake to ensure even layers

▶ Wrap tightly with the waxed paper and then with cellophane

Dining With the Dollar Diva

wrap and and put in freezer

▶ Let cake harden, remove and frost and return to freezer.

▶ Set cake out to thaw slightly from freezer, unwrap, frost cake with cake frosting, re-wrap to ensure easy cutting to serve. May use extra strawberries for decoration (mixed berries, may too runny for presentation), or serve with additional berries and whipped cream

$DIVA FYI

$ If you are unable to get the loaf pound cakes at $1 Store, use a box cake mix, from either your local supermarket or $1 Store.

Divalicious Menus with Ingredients Costing $1 or Less

Mrs. Small's Crème Brule'

I belong to an organization at Bethel AME Church called the Sterling Club. Each month one of the members is responsible for hosting a meeting. If the meeting is scheduled for 6:00 or 6:30PM members will be served a full course meal. Everything from soup to nuts. A 7PM meeting will just be dessert. I remember going to my first meeting at Mrs. Mary Smalls' home. I believe that even then, almost 20 years ago Mrs. Small was our oldest member, but girlfriend had, and still has, the energy, stamina and zest for life of anyone half her age. Anyway.....that meeting at Mrs. Small made me realize that when you sit down to a meal, you eat it twice. First with your eyes and then with your tastebuds. She had a "platter" of whole string beans where all of the string beans were the same length and were vertically lined up side by side. To this day, I still can't do that. At this that meeting, Mrs. Small had these carefully scooped balls of ice cream to top her homemade strawberry shortcake, and she didn't stop there. Mrs. Small gave us a choice of the strawberry shortcake or crème Brule that she prepared in individual ramekins. Sorry I got side tracked. As much as we enjoyed the beautifully sculptured shortcake whenever Mrs. Small has club meeting, everyone pretty much demands her legendary crème Brule as our dessert. Try this quick elegant dessert recipe. It's not Mrs. Small's but it ain't not bad!!!!!

INGREDIENTS
Instant French vanilla pudding Mix....................................<$1

½ cup milk ....Pantry or $1

3 egg yolks...Pantry or $1

¼ tsp nutmeg ....Pantry or $1

2 tbsp sugar...Pantry or $1

pinch of salt ....Pantry or $1

4 French vanilla pudding snack cups ......10-4-$10 or $1 or <$1

1 capful rum or vanilla extract.............................Pantry or $1

DIRECTIONS
▶ Set oven to 350 degrees

▶ Whisk pudding mix, milk, egg yolks, sugar and nutmeg together thoroughly

▶ Fold the 4 snack cups into pudding and egg mixture

▶ Add extract

▶ Pour into lightly greased baking dish/ramekin

▶ Place baking dish/ramekin in a deep pan, then fill with hot water (water bath)

▶ Place in oven bake for 25 minutes at 325 degrees

▶ Then increase temp and cook for another 20 minutes at 375

▶ Turn oven off when crème Brule is firm to touch and let crème brule sit in water bath in the oven until cool

▶ Remove pie from oven and lightly sprinkle top of pie with sugar

▶ Set oven on broiler, wait until oven is hot or broiler comes on

▶ Place pie on higher rack (not necessary to put on the top rack)

▶ Remove when sugar becomes caramelized. Keep eye on this as sugar will caramelize quickly, and your dessert will be ruined/burnt

▶ This can be served warm or cold

$Diva FYI

$ Substitute the French vanilla pudding mix and snack cups with butterscotch flavored pudding mix and butterscotch flavored snack cups.

$ Top with fresh fruit, not too much as you want to taste the crème brule.

Beignets w/Blackberry Sauce

I had a friend who was helping me clean up, paint and fix up my house for my Sterling Club meeting. He said that he was hungry and what was I fixing for lunch? I didn't know, but I knew that if I didn't feed him, I would be on

my own. I thought "Oh Nuts!!!!!" So, I went to the refrigerator, and my thoughts went from oh nuts to donuts!!! I saw the fixings for DONUTS!!! Once again, the refrigerated biscuits came to the rescue. This guy had plebian tastes, so he wouldn't have appreciated my calling these fried dough delicacies "beignets" nor the sauce that I included in this

recipe. I'm still searching for the tool to inject the filling into these recipes.

INGREDIENTS
    1 refrigerated biscuits
    (for these I would use the jumbo ones) ....10-4-$10
    1 c vegetable oil ....Pantry or $1
    1 c sugar ....Pantry or $1
    1/4 c nutmeg ....Pantry or $1
    1-6oz jar blackberry preserves

DIRECTIONS:
Blackberry Sauce
▶ Microwave blackberry preserves until melted
▶ Drizzle warm sauce over beignets and pour into a serving bowl/cup for dipping

Beignets

▶ Make sauce as the beignets fry extremely fast

▶ Place sugar and nutmeg in plastic container with lid or paper bag.

▶ In a deep sauce pan, heat oil on medium high

▶ Separate biscuits and cut into quarters and roll into tight balls

▶ Test oil to make sure ready for frying the beignets

▶ Lower heat to medium

▶ Place biscuits in oil, remove immediately when beignets become a light brown and/or float to top.

▶ Shake off excess oil

▶ Immediately place beignets in the lidded container or paper bag and shake to coat with nutmeg and sugar mixture.

▶ Remove and place on plate, if left in the covered container the beignets will get soft.

$1Diva FYI

$ Use fruit preserve, jam, or jelly of your choice, strawberry, raspberry, etc for dipping beignets.

$ Beignets are delicious when served warm, but can be served cold. Just make sure the blackberry sauce is warm!

Divalicious Menus with Ingredients Costing $1 or Less

$1 S'more Pie

I've never been much of a camper, so telling scary stories and roasting a graham cracker chocolate bar, marshmallow sandwich over a campfire just isn't appealing to me. But for some reason, s'mores kept calling my name. This recipe took some serious trial and error but I took a different spin on a childhood treat. I think you'll like this one!

INGREDIENTS

1 graham cracker crust $1

1 qt chocolate ice cream, softened.......................................$

½ bag marshmallows ....<$1

DIRECTIONS

▶ Pour softened ice cream into graham cracker crust

▶ Top with crushed chocolate bits (reserved some for garnish)

▶ Place in freezer until ice cream is firm

▶ When ice cream is firm top with marshmallow

▶ Place under broiler until marshmallows brown

▶ Serve immediately

Another quick indoor recipe for this campfire favorite is on the next page....

$1 Ovenbaked S'mores

INGREDIENTS
4 graham crackers broken in half $1
1 Chocolate bar $1
1 cup marshmallows...$1

DIRECTIONS
▶ Turn on broiler

▶ Place graham crackers on baking sheet

▶ Top 1/2 of graham crackers with the chocolate bar the other have cover with marshmallows

▶ Place under broil-er until marsh-mallows brown and chocolate softens (not di-rectly under broil-er so the graham crackers and marshmallows don't burn)

▶ Sprinkle chocolate chips over top of s'mores and allow to melt

▶ Serve immediately

$DIVA FYI

$ Watch s'mores carefully when under broiler to prevent burning.

$1 Focaccia Pineapple Cookie

When Marques was little we used to walk by those kiosk cookie shops in the mall that would have those really BIG cookies that could substitute for a cake or those pizza cookies were in vogue. Even then, Marques was a meat-and-potatoes man and he wasn't having any of that. Marques wanted a real cake or a real pizza; none of that would be a viable substitute. So with my baby a grown man, I though of a more mature take on the BIG/PIZZA cookie concept. Try for this dessert foccacia.

INGREDIENTS

1 package sugar cookie mix	$1
½ cup flaked coconut	$1
1 can pineapple tidbits, drained	$1
1-8 oz can tropical fruit, drained	<$1
1-6 oz jar strawberry or raspberry preserves	$1

1/2 jar maraschino cherries $1
1 3 oz bag walnuts $1
S2YT nutmeg & cinnamon ....Pantry or $1
S2YT Sugar ....Pantry or $1

DIRECTIONS

▶ Preheat oven 325 degrees

▶ Combine sugar cookie mix, coconut, cinnamon and/or nutmeg and in bowl and prepare according to package directions

▶ Roll out dough to a 12 inch round cookie

▶ Brush the strawberry/raspberry preserves on the entire cookie.

▶ Arrange pineapple and tropical fruit on top of cookie foccacia

▶ Cut maraschino cherries in half and place on top of cookie foccacia

▶ Bake for 25 minutes OR longer if you desire a crispy cookie

▶ Remove from oven

▶ Let cool slightly so cookie will chewy

$DIVA FYI

$ Substitute the maraschino cherries with dried cranberries.

$ Substitute the walnuts with your favorite nuts: almonds, pecans, and macadamia.

Divalicious Menus with Ingredients Costing $1 or Less

Brownies

My neighbor and walk buddy Debbie and I have made brownies a food group all of it's own. Some of my brownie recipes I can't put in this book unless you go to your local Wine and Spirits store and can get the airline bottles for 99¢. Then I got a few more brownie recipes to throw at ya. Maybe next book. Anyway…I would prefer using a brand chocolate brownie mix: I was able to buy a lot of boxes of a premium chocolate manufacturers brownie mix for 99 cents at a local discount grocery store chain." Believe it or not, I do favor the brand over the store name-brand!! Yeah, me Ms. Generic, I said that!!! Anyway, you will be able to get the brand brownie mix from the

$1 Store as well as your local grocery store, when it's available during a 10 for $10 sale. Trust me, here are some really good divalicious brownie recipes. Debbie and I have taste tested them numerous times!!!!

Divalicious Menus with Ingredients Costing $1 or Less

Milky Way Brownies

INGREDIENTS

1 box of brownie mix ....$1 or 10-4-$10

1 egg ....Pantry or $1

¼ oil...Pantry or $1

2 tsp milk ....Pantry or $1

1 tsp vanilla extract ....Pantry or $1

1-8 count pack mini Milky Way bars ....$1 or 10-4-$10

DIRECTIONS

▶ Preheat oven to 325 degrees

▶ Lightly grease baking dish

▶ Prepare fudge-like brownie mix according to directions on package

▶ Melt Milky Way bars in microwave at low temperature for 40 seconds. If you notice the edges are getting hard stir in in a little bit of oil or honey. And continue microwaving if candy bars are not completely melted.

▶ Stir melted Milky Way bars into the brownie mixture.

▶ Pour brownies into baking pan and bake according to package directions.

▶ When finished baking remove from oven

▶ Let cool for about five minutes

▶ Then cut

For a real Milky Way flavor, melt another pack of Milky Way bars and pour over top of brownies.

Butterfinger Brownies

INGREDIENTS
1 box of brownie mix ....$1 or 10-4-$10

1 egg ....Pantry or $1

¼ c oil ....Pantry or $1

2 tsp water

1 tsp vanilla extract ....Pantry or $1

8 mini Butterfingers bars ....$1 or 10-4-$10

DIRECTIONS
▶ Preheat oven to 325 degrees

Lightly grease baking pan

▶ Prepare Cake-like brownie mix according to directions on package

▶ Crumble Butterfinger candy bar and fold to brownie mixture.

▶ Pour brownie batter into lightly greased baking pan and bake according to package directions

▶ Let cool for about 5 minutes

▶ Then cut.

$1 Diva FYI:

$ Okay to frost but may have too much going on if you add an additional flavor dimension.

$ Can substitute with M&Ms or York Peppermint Patties.

German Chocolate Brownies

INGREDIENTS

1 box of brownie mix w/walnuts ....$1 or 10-4-$10

2 eggs ....Pantry or $1

¼ oil...Pantry or $1

1 tsp vanilla extract ....Pantry or $1

milk ....Pantryor $1

1-1/4 cup coconut ....Pantry or $1

1-8 count pkg Milky Way bar (optional) ....$1 or 10-4-$10

1-3 oz bag walnuts $1

1 container milk chocolate frosting $1

DIRECTIONS

▶ Preheat oven to 325 degrees

▶ Prepare cake-like brownie according to directions on package

▶ Melt Milky Way bars in microwave at low temperature for 40 seconds. If you notice the edges are getting hard, a little bit of milk or oil or honey to restore smoothness of the chocolate And continue microwaving if candy bars are not completely melted.

▶ Fold melted Milk Way bars, one half of coconut and one half of walnuts into brownie batter

▶ Pour brownie batter into lightly greased baking pan and bake according to package directions.

▶ When finished baking remove from oven

▶ Mix walnuts and coconut into frosting

▶ Let brownie cool for about five minutes, if you want the frosting to be a glaze, frost brownie while still warm: if you want the frosting to be more of an icing, then wait until brownie has cooled

If you prefer a heartier frosting, mix all of the coconut and walnuts into your frosting. OR Stir walnuts into the frosting and then top frosting with the remaining coconut. (Picture shown)

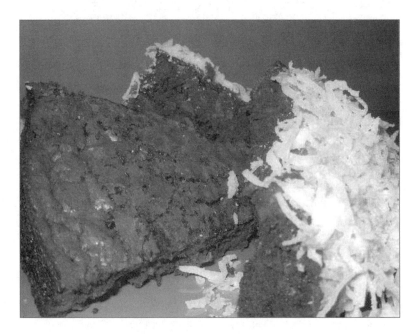

Divalicious Menus with Ingredients Costing $1 or Less

Cream Cheese Brownies

INGREDIENTS

1 box of brownie mix ....$1 or 10-4-$10

1 egg ....Pantry or $1

¼ c oil ....Pantry or $1

2 tsp water

1 tsp orange extract ....Pantry or $1

4 oz cream cheese ....$1 or <$1or 10-4-$10

1/2 c sugar ....Pantry or $1

DIRECTIONS

▶ Preheat oven to 325 degrees

▶ Lightly grease baking dish

▶ Prepare brownie mix according to directions on package for fudge like brownies (but this recipe also works well for the cake like brownies)

▶ Pour brownie batter into baking dish

▶ Pour brownie batter into lightly greased baking dish

▶ Using hand mixer whip sugar, vanilla, orange extract and cream cheese together until sugar is fully incorporated into the cream cheese

▶ Spoon cream cheese mixture randomly into the batter

▶ Bake according to package directions.

▶ Let cool for about five minutes before cutting

Oooeey Gooey Chocolate Brownies

INGREDIENTS

1 box of brownie mix ....$1 or 10-4-$10

2 eggs ....Pantry or $1

¼ c oil ....Pantry or $1

2 tsp water...Pantry or $1

¼ c chocolate sauce $1

½ c chocolate chips $1

DIRECTIONS

▶ Preheat oven to 325 degrees

▶ Lightly grease baking dish

▶ Prepare cake-like brownies according to directions on package

▶ Fold chocolate chips into brownie batter

▶ Pour brownie batter into lightly greased baking pan and bake according to package directions. You may need to add additional baking time because of chocolate chips

▶ Upon removing from oven, cool for one minute or two, then poke holes in brownie and then pour chocolate sauce over the entire brownie

▶ Serve warm with ice cream or whipped topping

$1 Diva FYI

$ Can substitute caramel or butterscotch sauce if you find this on sale.

Divalicious Menus with Ingredients Costing $1 or Less

Espresso Brownies

INGREDIENTS

1 box brownie mix ....$1 or 10-4-$10

1 egg ....Pantry or $1

¼ c oil...$1

2 tsp water

1 tsp vanilla extract ....Pantry or $1

1 tsp lemon extract or lemon zest ....Pantry or $1

1 individual packet mix of instant coffee or espresso $1

DIRECTIONS

▶ Preheat oven to 325 degrees

▶ Lightly grease baking dish

▶ Prepare fudge-like brownies according to directions on package, add instant coffee or espresso

▶ Pour brownies into baking pan and bake according to package directions

$Diva FYI

$ If you prefer your brownies strong, increase the amount of instant coffee or expresso.

$ Use of the lemon extract/lemon zest is a nice touch and brings out the coffee/espresso flavor.

Peach Fritters

God blessed me again!!! This recipe came to me as I was sitting in the choir box during the Main Line Black Interdenominal Ministerial Alliance Revival. Maybe I need to join a choir that sings all year long and I'll always have recipes! God forgive me. Hallelujah!!!

INGREDIENTS

1 box biscuit mix	$1
1 jar sliced peaches–diced	$1 or <$1
1 cup oil	Pantry or $1
S2YT nutmeg/cinnamon	Pantry or $1
½ c powdered sugar	Pantry or $1
1 tsp baking powder	Pantry or $1

DIRECTIONS

▶ Preheat saucepan with oil

▶ Place on medium high heat

▶ Drain peaches and dice

▶ Mix biscuit mix according to drop biscuit recipe

▶ Fold peaches into fritter mixture

▶ Spoon fitters into 1" balls and place carefully into hot oil

▶ Remove when they become golden brown and/or float to top

▶ Keep a constant eye on the fritters as they will brown quickly. To ensure they cook all the way through use a spoon and turn over in oil several times

▶ Drain on paper towel and sprinkle with powdered sugar immediately so sugar will stick to fritter.

$1 Diva FYI

$ May be served hot or cold.

$ Substitute pineapples, blueberries, apples, cranberries and/or chopped nuts.

$ For a savory fritter add chopped/minced garlic and diced onions to the bixicuit mix and substitute fruit with chopped clams, smoked oysters, or cooked diced pork roll.

Sweet Potato Biscuits

Remember that I am an AME, so when I refer to my Pastor/Minister, it may not be the current one or the same one. So...about 12 years ago, my Pastor's wife hosted a First Ladies District Conference Meeting at our church. This particular First Lady didn't spend much time in Bethel's kitchen with the kitchen committee nor with other members, but I heard on that particular day that the Pastor's wife put on a spread to beat the band. The star of the menu was her mouthwatering and lighter than air sweet potato biscuits. When I approached her and told her about the abundant compliments about her sweet potato biscuits, she just smiled. No, she didn't cough up the recipe, though. So I tried numerous times to make sweet potato biscuits from scratch. It just didn't work. So when I noticed the $1 Store selling biscuit mix, I grabbed a can of sweet potatoes from my pantry and tried this. Not too shabby!!! Yes, the canned sweets cost less than $1.00, but you could also use one large fresh sweet potato, which would also cost under $1.00. I've tried this on numerous occasions. If you use the canned mashed sweet potatoes there is no need to drain them, but you'll have to adjust the amount of sugar to your desired sweetness. If you use the candied sweet potatoes, you'll have to drain them. So adjust your sugar accordingly as these will be sweeter than the mashed canned potatoes.

INGREDIENTS

1-18.5 oz all purpose biscuit mix.......................................$1

½ cup sugar ....Pantry or $1

3/4 cup milk ....Pantry or $1

2 egg..Pantry or $1

¼ tsp cinnamon ....Pantry or $1

1 tsp baking powder ....Pantry or $1

Canned sweet potatoes (drain if using canned candied sweets)

DIRECTIONS

▶ Preheat oven to 325 degrees, and lightly grease baking sheet

▶ Drain and mash sweet potatoes

▶ In mixing bowl, combine biscuit mix, baking powder cinnamon and sugar together

▶ In a separate bowl mix mashed sweet potatoes along with milk and eggs

▶ Mix wet and dry ingredients until your dough is incorporated

▶ Biscuit dough may be sticky as a result of using sweet potato, so you may need to add additional mix.

▶ Knead dough on a floured surface (I add a little bit of sugar to the floured surface)

▶ Don't over knead

▶ Cut into round biscuits

▶ Place on lightly greased baking sheet

▶ Bake for approx 25 minutes or until brown

▶ Remove from oven and brush tops with melted butter

▶ Sprinkle with sugar

$1 Store Apricot Scones

Usually when I get my walk on, I hang with my neighbor and walk buddy Debbie, my neighbor from across the street. We get to the corner of our block, we turn and look at one another, and then point—which way, Villanova or Ardmore?? More often than not, we end up going towards Ardmore, because we can stop at the local supermarket and do a mini-food shop or........there is this drop-your-jaw-make-you-slap-your-ownself bakery across the street from the grocery store that has the most absolutely delicious baked goods that you ever want to eat. My personal favorites are their lemon squares and their scones. Hmmmmm......yes, I have a lemon square recipe all ready for you. But this is scone time.

INGREDIENTS
    1 package biscuit mix $1
    1 cup milk ....Pantry or $1
    ½ cup dried apricots $1
    ½ cup sugar ....Pantry or $1
    ¼ cup melted butter ....Pantry or $1

DIRECTIONS
▶ Preheat oven 375 degrees

▶ Combine biscuit mix, sugar and apricots together

▶ Then add milk and prepare according to package directions. (I did notice that with some of the $1 Store brands biscuit mix, the dough tends to be real wet, so I suggest that you reduce the amount of liquid required, but if you are able to purchase a brand name, follow the "rolled dough" biscuit directions.)

▶ Knead dough on a floured surface (I add a little bit of sugar to the flour.)

▶ Roll out dough into a 9x12 rectangle, cut into 12 smaller rectangles, and cut each smaller rectangle diagonally in half

▶ Place on greased baking sheet

▶ Bake according to package directions

Divalicious Menus with Ingredients Costing $1 or Less

▶ Brush melted butter on top of each scone and immediately sprinkle with sugar

▶ Let cool slightly, serve with butter and jam or eat plain

$1 Diva FYI

$ I prefer eating the scones hot/warm, but you can serve cold along with your favorite tea and/or coffee. I've also tried the recipe with cranberries, raisins, and nuts. Be creative.

$ Debbie suggested that I use chocolate chips. I told her that chocolate chips go in cookies and brownies, not scones or muffins, but hey, I keep saying be creative, right?

Dining With the Dollar Diva

Frosted Dolla'Bons

I have always been a Cinnabon® fan. I remember when the Cinnabon franchises started popping up everywhere in the southeastern PA areas— King of Prussia, St. Davids, at 3oth Street Station, University City. I mean everywhere. What was so exciting was the theatrical performance that was put on by the Cinnabon maker. He or she would roll out the pastry dough, making sure that it was in compliance with the perfect rectangular template. Then there would be 1lb blocks of margarine in a pyramid display, and then they would sprinkle on the sugar and the exotic aroma of Makara cinnamon. Then the pastry maker would slowly roll the sugar-n-spice butter laden dough lengthwise making sure that with each roll, the dough, the entire length, was the same width. Then using a yard stick, he would make sure that each cinnamon bun is the same $1^{1}/_{2}$ size. Then these cinnamony delicacies would be placed gingerly in the pan and put into the timer ovens. People would wait the seven minutes for the rolls and often times you could request more frosting on your individual roll. Now the majority of the stores are FTO's (Freezer to Oven) and you don't have the luxury of seeing the show. No more long lines waiting for the beautiful presentation. Now, I just enjoy the fragrance walking by the Cinnabon kiosk and go home and make my own divalicious Dolla'bons!!!

INGREDIENTS
1 can refrigerated biscuits, (for these I would get the
large sized buttermilk ones not the flakey) ....10-4-$10
$1^{1}/_{2}$ stick softened margarine ....<$1
$1^{1}/_{2}$ c brown sugar...$1
$1^{1}/_{2}$ c white sugar $1
2 tbsp cinnamon ....Pantry or $1
2 tbsp nutmeg ....Pantry or $1

PREPEARATION DIRECTIONS
▶ Preheat oven to 350 degrees
▶ Flour your surface and lay the biscuits in 2 rows of 4 (over lap)

Divalicious Menus with Ingredients Costing $1 or Less

▶ Roll until about 1/2 " thick, on a floured surface. There
 may/will be spaces between the biscuits. Just pinch together,
 for the stubborn ones. Dab with water over the ends and then
 roll. They should stick.

▶ Spread a generous layer of margarine over the dough. Believe it
 or not, the margarine is better for the inside spice layer. Save
 the butter for the frosting

▶ Leave a ¼" non-buttered edge

▶ In bowl, mix the brown and white sugars, and add your
 cinnamon and nutmeg. Use a shortening cutter to make sure
 there are no lumps

▶ Layer generously on the buttered dough. Don't forget to leave a
 ¼ edge

▶ Start rolling the dough length wise, using wax paper as a guide. When you get to the end of rolling the dolla'bon dough, have the seam side facing upwards. This will make it easier to remove from refrigerator after "resting" and will facilitate cutting.

▶ Now, you can either keep the dollabon roll in wax paper and let it rest in the refrigerator and later cut into 2" widths or cut immediately and bake. Although these do spread, I like mine to really rise close together, so when placing the rolls in the pan, have them touch slightly.

▶ Bake for approximately 30-45 minutes depending on oven.

Below are 3 different frostings you can make while the cinnamon buns are cooking

8 oz cream cheese

1 ½ c powdered sugar

▶ Mix until it is a smooth consistency

1 stick of butter (must be butter)

2 cups confectioner's sugar

▶ Microwave butter, stir in sugar until you get the consistency desired, glaze, thin/thick frosting

▶ Or just purchase a can of frosting. It's only $1 at the dollar store

Peach Melba

This is a very easy dessert to shop for and prepare. The elegance is in how you display the ingredients in the bowl or goblet that you use to serve it in. Remember, you'll eat this one with your eyes first. Carefully arrange peaches on top sides for artful display. Your guests will be impressed with your epicurean skills.

INGREDIENTS

1 can peaches ....<$1

1 yellow pound cake sliced $1

Pudding <$1 or ice cream $1

Whipped cream ....$1 or <$1

DIRECTIONS

▶ Place a layer of pound cake in the bottom of the glass bowl

▶ Layer with pudding or ice cream

▶ Layer peaches

▶ Repeat layering process until cake is top layer

▶ Top final layer with whipped cream and a sprig of mint and fruit

$DIVA FYI

$ If a pre-made pound cake is unavailable, use a yellow cake mix. Sprinkle nutmeg or cinnamon in batter before baking.

Ho-Jo Strawberry Shortcake

Going back in time again, if you remember Horn & Hardart, then you got to have memories about Howard Johnson's. Remember the family chain restaurant back in the '50's & 60's with the brilliant blue and orange color scheme? They were known for their the fried clam sandwiches, (I shoulda put that one in this book), and the best hamburgers and fries. Howard Johnson's had this really neat ice cream scooper that had a interesting rounded-square shape. They served just good wholesome food at reasonable prices. Sound familiar???? Anyway......

I have a story for this one too. Picture this.... June 1966, Swedeland Elementary School, my best-est friends and neighbors, Darryl Askew, Victoria Evans and I graduated from 6th grade. My parents were divorced by then, so, my father, who worked during the day was unable to come to my little graduation ceremony. Daddy called Mommy and told her that he would like to take me and my buddies out for "eeerrts". (Now you do know the "eerrts story" from my previous H&H vignettes, don't you?) Mommy called Miss Tillie and Mrs. Askew to let them know that Daddy wanted to take Darryl and Vicki to Howard Johnson's, and their parents agreed to the outing!!!. A few days later, Daddy showed up at 257 Kentucky in his white panel van, and the three of us trotted out ready for an adventure. When we got to Howard Johnson's the hostess showed us to our booth, and the famous orange and blue color scheme dazzled us. The three of us felt very grown up when the waitress gave us the "grown up adult" menus instead of the children's menu. Immediately, Darryl and I ordered hamburgers and French fries, and Vicki being the perfect child

Divalicious Menus with Ingredients Costing $1 or Less

that she always was, ordered the dessert that she was supposed to. I still remember the look on my father's face when he heard Darryl and I order a meal instead of a dessert.

Well... Darryl and I got our hamburger platters, but when the waitress placed that monstrous strawberry shortcake (served in king size milkshake glasess) in front of Vicki, I looked at Darryl, Darryl looked at me, and my Father rolled his eyes in back of his head, knowing that not only was he in for paying for two hamburger platters for Darryl and me, he knew that he was going to be out of pocket for another two additional strawberry shortcakes. Being the kind-hearted man that he was, when Darryl and I ordered our dessert, Daddy told the waitress to bring another strawberry shortcake for Vicki!!! We had a wonderful time.

Although the Fisher's strawberry shortcake was strawberries, a biscuit and whipped cream, I kinda got used to Ho-Jo's strawberry shortcake recipe: cake, layer of strawberries, scoop of ice cream, another layer of strawberries, and a humongous dollop of whipped cream. Just like this picture. That was a wonderful time that I spent with three of my most favorite people.

INGREDIENTS/DIRECTIONS:
▶ Follow the same directions as the peach melba recipe, but use a bag of strawberries instead of peaches. Pleasing to the eye served in a tall milkshake glass or a chic goblet.

Chocolate Fondue

I was on a two week vacation with my son, Marques in Warner Robins, GA when I tried to make frozen chocolate covered bananas. First, let me say that I have a new found respect for those kids who work in custard stands across the country serving up this frozen chocolate fruit treat. I don't know if it's all in the wrist, or you have a special banana flown in from Brazil, but my bananas didn't look too appealing, and I added insult to injury and tried just covering them with chopped nuts. It was a true disaster, but I didn't want to let all of that chocolate deliciousness go to waste, and what would I do with the skewers that I bought for the bananas? Hmmm... Marques' local grocery store had a ton of fresh fruit on sale for 99cents/lb, strawberries, oranges, grapes, etc. so I put them on skewers along with the mini donuts that were two for 78 cents, and that's how this decadent fondue was made out of what could have been one hot chocolate mess. So not only was the fondue dolla-rific, the dippers were even less. So I'm still adhering to my less than $1 ingredient concept and still being health conscious.

PS: I know, the corresponding picture looks like a cup of black coffee, but it is an extraordinary chocolate self-indulgence fondue where all of the ingredients can be purchased for a $1 or less (fruit was 99 cents/lb) or your choice of "dippers" all can be purchased at the dollar store as well.

INGREDIENTS
½ bag chocolate chips $1
½ cup chocolate syrup $1
1 tsp vanilla ....Pantry or $1
2 tsp heavy cream..$1

DIRECTIONS
▶ Use a double boiler or place a metal bowl on top of a larger size pot ¾ filled with water

▶ Bring water to simmer

▶ Do NOT allow bottom of bowl to be submerged in water, and water should NOT boil

▶ Put your "dippers" on skewers

▶ Place all of the ingredients in bowl/top boiler pan

▶ Keep eye on the chocolate

▶ Begin to stir when you notice chocolate chips start to melt

▶ When chocolate is completely melted, remove from heat

▶ Don't allow to over heat as chocolate will seize

▶ Pour chocolate fondue into a serving bowl

▶ Arrange dippers around bowl on separate platter

▶ Everyone can choose their own or allow each person their own dish with assorted dippers

$DIVA FYI

$ FoodNetwork hostess Gia DeLaurentis adds a little bit of honey when she melts her chocolate. So, be on the look out for honey at $1 Store or the 10-4-$10 sales.

Frozen Bananas

I've included the recipe that I was going to use for the frozen bananas. Please try it. I'll relish in the fact that I had some involvement with your victorious success with this recipe. Julia Child said that you never have to apologize for food. But sometimes things just don't work out the way you want them to. This was one of those times. Bon Appétit!!!

INGREDIENTS

3 firm bananas, sliced in half $1

½ c chocolate sauce $1

½ bag chocolate chips $1

2 tbs butter ....Pantry or <$1

1 small individual size bag of peanuts..............................<$1

Popsicle sticks (find in arts and crafts store or school supply area in $1)/skewers $1

DIRECTIONS

▶ Line baking pan with wax paper (spray lightly with spray oil)

▶ Fill bowl with chocolate sauce

▶ Crush peanuts and spread in even layer on a large flat surface/plate

▶ Peel bananas, sliced in half (cross section)

▶ Insert popsicle sticks halfway into banana

▶ Dip banana into chocolate sauce

▶ Hold downward over board

▶ Let excess drip off

▶ Then roll into peanuts

▶ Place on baking pan

▶ Repeat process until all banana halves are coated

▶ Place in freezer until frozen

▶ Serve frozen

$1 Diva FYI

$ Don't use overly ripe bananas.

$ Work fast so bananas don't turn brown, or squeeze lemon on bananas to prevent them turning brown.

$ Try using the chocolate fondue recipe for coating the bananas. Then freeze.

Fellowship Bread

For some reason, I could not bring myself to call anything I eat Monkey Bread. I know that there must be a story behind it, but I just can't do it. So….since my recipe made its debut during Bethel AME Ardmore's repasts after one of their Sunday worship services, I'm calling it this sticky, gooey, cinnamonny pastry Fellowship Bread.

INGREDIENTS:

1 can jumbo refrigerated biscuit dough ....10-4-$10

1½ stick of butter (because the refrigerated biscuits have a distinct flavor, I would NOT use margarine) ....10-4-$10

2 cups of white sugar ....Pantry or $1

2 cups of brown sugar ....Pantry or $1

2 tbsp cinnamon ....Pantry or $1

2 tbsp nutmeg ....Pantry or $1

1-6 oz box raisins (Optional) $1

1 3 oz bag walnuts...$1

DIRECTIONS:

▶ Preheat oven to 325 degrees

▶ Butter the pan or baking dish that you are going to use. Keep in mind that these biscuits RISE so make sure that the baking dish or pan you are using can accommodate the number of biscuits you are going to use

▶ If you are using raisins & nuts in this recipe, sprinkle the raisins and nuts in the bottom of baking dish

▶ Microwave butter in a deep, flat bottom bowl or large measuring cup

▶ Mix the two sugars, pour a little bit of the melted butter into the baking dish to coat bottom, and mix in cinnamon & nutmeg together in a pie pan or large plate

▶ Separate the biscuits, cut into quarters, and roll each one into a tight ball

Divalicious Menus with Ingredients Costing $1 or Less

▶ Drop the biscuit balls into the melted butter, make sure that each one is coated thoroughly

▶ Roll into the sugar and spice mixture

▶ Make sure that each one is coated thoroughly, place into baking dish/pan.

▶ When you have one complete layer, sprinkle some raisins and nuts

▶ Repeat until all of the biscuit balls have been buttered and sugared

▶ Let sit for about five minutes (kinda let them rise a bit). Then sprinkle the remaining sugar mixture and pour the remaining butter over what will be the bottom layer of the bread

▶ Put in oven and bake for about 20-25 minutes. Let sit for a minute or two

▶ Place large plate gently on top of the Fellowship Bread, and carefully invert

$1 Diva FYI

$ Bottom of fellowship bread will be a bit hard, but after a while of baking, of the sugar and butter will become syrup-like. And after inverting the bread, the syrup will ooze to the bottom.

$ Let set for just a minute and use your hands to pull apart and enjoy, but if you can't wait for them to cool, use a fork to pull each ball away.

Baked Alaska

Believe it or not, I really didn't pay much attention to Mrs. Junger, my Junior High Home Economics teacher. I don't understand why, because the two things she taught were the things that I enjoyed the most back then: cooking, eating, and sewing. Another story on the sewing part. But anyway, there were several dishes that Mrs. Junger had us cook. She gave us the basics for this besmel (white sauce) that she used for nearly everything we cooked that year, except for the impressive baked Alaska. Now again, that was over 40 years ago, so my memory could be a little bit clouded. But for some bizarre reason, I remember the first time she made it in our class. She only made a serving for herself, and she made it with a half of a grapefruit instead of using a cake base. Well, I went right home and made it for myself. Yeah, I ate about 6 pieces, but remember back then that food was one of my best-est friends. Heck, it still is!!!! But here's a different take off of this most elegant dessert. Use marshmallows for the meringue and use different flavored ice creams for a more spectacular presentation.

INGREDIENTS
    1 quart Neapolitan ice cream..$1
    1 pound cake loafs $1
    1 bag large sized marshmallows.......................................<$1

DIRECTIONS:
   ▶ Lightly grease your deep baking dish (make sure your baking dish can go from freezer to oven)
   ▶ Line with plastic wrap or wax paper, and make sure there is enough to make handles that overlap edges
   ▶ Slice pound cake in half, and place in oven safe baking dish. Pace the rounded top half cut side down in the baking dish
   ▶ Place scoops of ice cream over the pound cake
   ▶ Cover with plastic wrap and put in freezer until frozen
   ▶ Remove baked Alaska when cake and ice are frozen

Divalicious Menus with Ingredients Costing $1 or Less

▶ Place baked Alaska on cookie sheet and cover with marshmallows

▶ Before serving, set oven on BROIL

▶ Place under broiler

▶ Do not leave unattended

▶ Remove when marshmallows reach desired browness

▶ Let set for a minute for easier cutting

▶ Serve

$DIVA FYI

$ If pound cake is not available, purchase a box yellow cake mix. Prepare cake mix according to the directions on the package. TIP: Stir a tsp of nutmeg in batter before baking a 9"x9" square pan.

$ Allow cake to cool before assembling the baked Alaska.

Notes

Divalicious Menus with Ingredients Costing $1 or Less

Notes

_____

_____

_____

_____

_____

_____

_____

_____

_____

_____

_____

_____

_____

_____

_____

_____

_____

_____

_____

_____

_____

_____

_____

_____

_____

Dining With the Dollar Diva

Glossary

Add	To mix or stir in the ingredients listed in the instructions.
Adjust seasonings	Always taste food before you add more seasonings. You can add, but you can't remove, too much seasoning.
Batter	A mixture of flour, milk, eggs, sugar, and butter. Mixture textures will vary, all batters must be thin enough to pour.
Beat	To introduce air into a mixture by beating rapidly with a wooden spoon, wire whisk or electric mixer until batter is very smooth.
Bisque	A creamed or puréed soup with additions of fish or vegetables.
Blend	To combine ingredients in an electric blender or food processor or to mix ingredients of different textures into a smooth mixture. A blender is best used for puréed soups, sauces, drinks, and salad dressings. A food processor works better with solid liquid ingredients and handles chopping, grating, shredding and makes pastry dough.
Boil	To heat a liquid until bubbles rise rapidly to the surface. A rolling boil occurs when bubbles rise to the surface vigorously.
Brand names	Well-known manufactured product items.
Broil	To cook food on a broiler pan 2-3 inches from the radiant element in oven.
Broth/stock	The liquid which results from the simmering of meat, poultry, vegetables, or bones with seasonings, herbs and vegetables.
Brown	To caramelize, fry or sauté food on medium high to high heat in order to develop a rich color on the outside and

Divalicious Menus with Ingredients Costing $1 or Less

add flavor to the dish.

Caramelize	When cooking vegetables and/or fruits, the sugars are broken down and become brown and produce a nutty-like flavor and delicious aromas.
Chill	To cool a food in the refrigerator or freezer.
Chop	Cutting food into smaller pieces on a cutting board.
Deglaze	To loosen pan drippings in a hot skillet/pan by stirring in liquid.
Diced	Ingredients which have been cut into uniform pieces
Dredge	To coat meat/vegetables with flour, cornmeal or cornstarch prior to frying or baking.
Drippings	The residual fat and meat pieces remaining in pan after meat has been roasted or fried.
Drizzle	To pour/drip icing in a thin stream over a cake or pastry
Drop	To allow a batter, dough, or a mixture to fall from a spoon onto the area that will cook it.
Egg wash	An egg and water or egg and milk mixture that is brushed over breads or pastry before baking.
Fold	To slowly and lightly mix a lighter mixture with a heavier one. such as cake batter, without releasing air bubbles. Use a vertical motion.
Frosting/Icing	Sweet coating for cakes, breads or cookies.
Fry	To cook food in oil or butter over medium-high heat
Garnish	The process of decorating and adding visual appeal to dishes of prepared food with edible foods (zests, seasonings/spices, fresh herbs, etc.).
Grease	To coat a pan with some type of shortening; butter, margarine, oil or fat.
Herbs	Herbs come from the aromatic leaves of many plants.
Hors d'oeuvre	Appetizers and portions of savory foods served with toothpicks or eaten as finger food.

Dining With the Dollar Diva

Hot Water Bath	A dish is set in a larger pan and water is poured around dish to be baked.
Invert	To turn a food upside down prior to serving,
Macerate	To soften vegetables or fruits soft by soaking in a liquid.
Margarine	May substitute this shortening for butter.
Melt	To turn solid food into a semi-liquid by applying low heat. This is a term used often in connection with shortenings (butter, margarine, or solid vegetable shortening) and chocolate.
Minced	To chop meats, vegetables, herbs, as finely as possible.
Mix	Stir with a spoon or fork so that the ingredients are evenly distributed.
Moisten	To add enough liquid to a dry ingredient to make it damp.
Pinch	The amount of a dry ingredient you can hold between tips of the thumb and index finger.
Preheat	The process of turning on oven so that it will be at the recommended temperature to cook a food by the time the food has been prepared. This is especially important when baking cakes or roasting meats.
Ramekins	Small glazed ceramic serving bowls built to withstand high temperatures, as they are frequently used in ovens.
Recipe	A recipe is a list of ingredients with instructions. This is a starting point for your own creativity.
Reduce	To decrease the quantity of a liquid by simmering a liquid, such as beef stock, in an uncovered pan until the quantity is noticeably decreased and the flavor concentrated.
Roasting	Place meat fat side up on in a shallow or deep roasting pan for cooking in an oven.
Roll	To use a rolling pin to flatten dough or pastry.
Roux	Cooked mixture of flour and melted shortening/fat, butter, margarine or oil. It is the thickening agent for

Divalicious Menus with Ingredients Costing $1 or Less

	sauces, gravies andstews. The butter is melted and then the flour is whisked into thebutter. A liquid is added to form a sauce, gravy or soup. An excellent base for white (béchamel) sauce.
Sauté	Method of cooking food that uses a small amount of oil/shortening in a shallow pan over high heat. The food that is sautéed is browned while preserving its texture, moisture and flavor.
Seize	Properly melted chocolate should have a smooth and satiny appearance. If it comes into contact with a small amount of water, it will "seize," or turn into a grainy, clumpy mess in the bowl. If chocolate is overheated, it will be quite thick and lumpy.
Shortening	This is a vegetable oil which has been processed to form a solid form used for baking and frying.
Simmer	To cook a liquid over low heat without boiling. Simmer is sometimes called a "gentle boil." Small bubbles rise to the surface - the gentler and slower the bubbles, the lower the temperature of what is being cooked.
Skillet	A thick-based fry pan; the thick base allows the heat to spread evenly.
Skim	To remove fat or foam from the surface of a beverage, soup or sauce with a spoon. This can also be done after a soup has been chilled. The congealed fat can then be easily lifted off.
Slice	To cut food into thick or thin slices.
Spices	Spices come from the seeds, bark, fruit, flower or roots of plants and add dimension to foods.
Sprinkle	Dusting a fine powdery layer over food or a cooking surface.
Stir	To blend ingredients using a spoon or fork in a circular motion.

Dining With the Dollar Diva

Stir-fry	A quick method of cooking in a wok over high heat. The wok is heated and the vegetables and meats are stirred to cook quickly.
Stock	The flavorful liquid produced when meats, herbs and vegetables are simmered for a long time.
Thaw	To unfreeze a frozen food and bring it room temperature. Meats should be thawed in the refrigerator.
Toss	To gently mix ingredients using a large spoon and fork with a lifting motion then allow ingredients to drop back into bowl.
Whip	To beat rapidly to add air and increase volume of a cream or egg white mixture. Use a wire whisk or electric mixer.
Whisk	A looped wire kitchen utensil to mix in a fast circular motion.

Index

	$1 Store Sweet & Sour Chicken/Shrimp, 78
Brownie Mix	Butterfinger Brownies, 146
	Cream Cheese Brownies, 149
	Espresso Brownies, 151
	German Chocolate Brownies, 147
	Milky Way Brownies, 145
	Oooeey Gooey Chocolate Brownies, 150
Butterfinger Candy Bar	Butterfinger Brownies, 146
Cake Frosting	Frosted Dolla'Bons, 158
	Ice Cream Cake, 133
	Vanilla Napoleon Rounds, 126
Cake Mix	Baked Alaska, 170
	Ho-Jo Strawberry Shortcake, 162
	Ice Cream Cake, 133
	Peach Melba, 161
Carrots	$1 Store Sweet & Sour Chicken/Shrimp, 78
	Peas and Carrot Bisque, 111
Cheese	$1 Store Garlic Cheese Bread, Mozzarella, 66
	$1 Store Ravioli Carbonara, Muenster, 64
	Baked Eggs Florentine, Mozzarella, 69
	Hot Queso Dip with Tomatoes & Sausage, Velveeta, 19
	Inside Out Burgers, 52
	Macaroni and Cheese, Mozzarella, 104
	Mc$1 Store Eggs Benedict, 117
	Mini Quiches, 26
	Monte Cristo, 40
	Baked Muenster Cheese w/Orange Marmalade in Puffed Pastry, 6
	Oyster Stromboli, Mozzarella, 85
	Pepperoni & Swiss Knots, Swiss Cheese, 13
	Pescado Garlic Bread, Mozzarella, 17
	Pizza Squares, Mozzarella, Cheddar, 75
	Sausage Pinwheels, Mozzarella, Cheddar, 24
	Shrimp and Scallop Quesadilla, Cheddar, 45
	Southwest Chili Salad, Cheddar, 81
	Spicy Blue Cheese Dipping Sauce, Feta, 28
	Tilapia Rollups, Cottage Cheese, Mozzarella, 96
Cheese Dip	$1 Store Ravioli Carbonara, 64
	Baked Eggs Florentine, Mozzarella, 69
	Cheese Fondue, 23

Divalicious Menus with Ingredients Costing $1 or Less

	Macaroni and Cheese, 104
	Mc$1 Store Breakfast Sandwich, 44
	Mc$1 Store Eggs Benedict, 117
Chicken	Juliet's Chicken, 115
	Cream Chicken Mushroom Corn Chowder, 76
	$1 Store Sweet & Sour Chicken/Shrimp, 78
	Chicken Medallions, 12
	Chicken Sliders (Mini Chicken Sandwiches), 46
Chili	Southwest Chili Salad, 81
Chocolate Chips	Chocolate Fondue, 164
	Oooeey Gooey Chocolate Brownies, 150
Chocolate Sauce	Chocolate Fondue, 164
	Oooeey Gooey Chocolate Brownies, 150
	Vanilla Napoleon Rounds, 126
Clams	Clam Chowder, 87
	Peach Fritters, 152
Coconut	$1 Store Foccacia Pineapple Cookie, 141
	German Chocolate Brownies, 147
Coconut Milk	Peas & Carrot Bisque, 111
Coffee	Espresso Brownies, 151
Collard Greens	Cream of Tomato Soup w/Collard Greens & Blackbeans, 67
Corn	Southwest Chili Salad, 81
Cottage Cheese	Calzone, 83
	Oyster Stromboli, 85
	Ms. Jeri's Meatball Ravioli Lasagne, 91
	Sausage Pinwheels, 24
	Tilapia Rollups, 96
Cranberries	$1 Store Apricot Scones, 156
	$1 Store Foccacia Pineapple Cookie, 141
	Cinnamon Apple—Almond Raisin Waffle Panini, 43
	Empanadas, 15
	Peach Fritters, 152
Cream Cheese	Cream Cheese Brownies, 149
	Elder Denise's Lemon Berry Parfait, 130
	Frosted Dolla'bons, 158
	Pineapple & Salami Roll-ups, 7
	Vanilla Napoleon Rounds, 126
Cream of Celery Soup	Cream Chicken Mushroom Corn Chowder, 76
	Mock Lobster Pie, 108

Dining With the Dollar Diva

	Cream Chicken Mushroom Corn Chowder, 76
Cream of	
Mushroom Soup	Mock Lobster Pie, 108
	Cream Chicken Mushroom Corn Chowder, 76
Eggs	Baked Eggs Florentine, 69
	Mc$1 Store Breakfast Sandwich, 44
	Mc$1 Store Eggs Benedict, 117
English Muffins	Mc$1 Store Breakfast Sandwich, 44
	Mc$1 Store Eggs Benedict, 117
Espresso	Espresso Brownies, 151
Flounder	Fish Fried Rice, 114
	Mini Quiches, 26
	Mock Lobster Pie, 108
	Seafood Jambalaya, 94
Fruit Preserves	$1 Store Foccacia Pineapple Cookie, 141
	Beignets w/Blackberry Sauce, Black Currant, 137
	Marmalade Mayonnaise, Orange Marmalade, 29
	Monte Cristo, 40
	Baked Muenster Cheese w/Orange Marmalade in Puffed Pastry, 6
	Strawberry Preserves and Muenster Waffle Sandwich, 38
Graham Cracker	
Crust	$1 S'more Pie, 139
Graham Crackers	$1 Ovenbaked S'mores, 140
	Elder Denise's Lemon Berry Parfait, 130
Ground Turkey	Inside Out Burgers, 52
	Meatballs & Tuna Bites, 10
	Mini Quiches, 26
	Ms. Branda's Shepherd's Pie, 62
	Salisbury Steak, 101
	Salsa Burgers, 53
Ham	Cheese Fondue, 23
	Monte Cristo, 40
Honey	Peanut Butter & Bananas w/Honey Sandwich, 41
Horseradish Sauce	Chipolte-Wasabi Mayonnaise, 27
Hot Dogs	Hot Dogs and Spicy Sauerkraut, 72
Ice Cream	$1 S'more Pie, 139
	Baked Alaska, 170
	Ho-Jo Strawberry Shortcake, 162
	Ice Cream Cake, 133

Divalicious Menus with Ingredients Costing $1 or Less

Mixed Vegetables	Fish Fried Rice, 114
	Ms. Branda's Shepherd's Pie, 62
Mushrooms	$1 Store Sweet & Sour Chicken/Shrimp, 78
	Clam Chowder, 87
	Cream Chicken Mushroom Corn Chowder, 76
	Fish Fried Rice, 114
	Mock Lobster Pie, 108
	Oyster Stew, 89
	Oyster Stromboli, 85
	Salisbury Steak, 101
	Seafood Jambalaya, 94
Mustard	$1 Store Lobster Rolls, Dijon, 36
	Curry Mayonnaise, Dijon, 28
Onion Soup Mix	Salisbury Steak, 101
Orange Juice	$1 Store Sweet & Sour Chicken/Shrimp, 78
Orange Marmalade	Marmalade Mayonnaise, 29
	Baked Muenster Cheese w/Orange Marmalade in Puffed Pastry, 6
Oysters	$1 Store Po' Boy, 48
	Peach Fritters, 152
	Oyster Stew, 89
	Oyster Stromboli, 85
Pasta	$1 Store Ravioli Carbonara, 64
	Macaroni and Cheese, Rigatoni, 104
	Tilapia Rollups, Lasagne Noodles, 96
Peaches	Fruit Tart, 128
	Peach Fritters, 152
	Peach Melba, 161
Peanut Butter	Peanut Butter & Bananas w/Honey Sandwich, 41
Pears	Fruit Tart, 128
	Peach Fritters, 152
Peas and Carrots	Oyster Stew, 89
	Peas and Carrot Bisque, 111
Pepperoni	Pepperoni & Swiss Knots, 13
	Pineapple Salami Roll-up, 7
Peppers	$1 Store Lobster Rolls, 36
	$1 Store Sweet & Sour Chicken/Shrimp, 78
	Chipolte-Wasabi Mayonnaise, Chipolte, 28
	Hot Queso Dip with Tomatoes & Sausage, Jalapenos, 19

Divalicious Menus with Ingredients Costing $1 or Less

	Prickly Relish, pepperoncini, 28
	Shrimp and Scallop Quesadilla, 45
	Southwest Chili Salad, 81
	Tilapia Rollups, 96
Pie Crust	Apple Dumpling w/Warm Custard Sauce, 106
	Fruit Tart, 128
	Baked Muenster Cheese w/Orange Marmalade in Puffed Pastry, 6
	Oyster Stromboli, 85
	Vanilla Napoleon Rounds, 126
Pineapple	$1 Store Foccacia Pineapple Cookie, 141
	$1 Store Sweet & Sour Chicken/Shrimp, 78
	Pineapple & Salami Roll-up, 7
	Fruit Tart, 128
	Peach Fritters, 152
Pizza Crust	Pizza Squares, 75
	Sausage Pinwheels, 24
Pork Roll	$1 Store Ravioli Carbonara, 64
	Mc$1 Store Breakfast Sandwich, 44
Potatoes	Clam Chowder, 87
	Ms. Branda's Shepherd's Pie, Mashed/Instant, 62
	Oyster Stew, 89
	Peas & Carrot Bisque, 111
Pound Cake	Baked Alaska, 170
	Ho-Jo Strawberry Shortcake, 162
	Ice Cream Cake, 133
	Peach Melba, 161
Puffed Pastry	Baked Muenster Cheese w/Orange Marmalade in Puffed Pastry, 6
Raisin	$1 Store Apricot Scones, 156
	Cinnamon Apple—Almond Raisin Waffle Panini, 43
	Empanadas, 15
	Fellowship Bread, 168
	Tea Biscuits, 105
Ravioli	$1 Store Ravioli Carbonara, 64
	Ms. Jeri's Meatball Ravioli Lasagne, 91
Refrigerated Biscuit Dough	Beignets w/Blackberry Sauce, 137
	Frosted Dolla'bons, 158
	Empanadas, 158
	Fellowship Bread, 168

𝒟ining With the 𝒟ollar 𝒟iva

	Mini Quiches, 26
	Mock Lobster Pie, 108
	Ms. Branda's Shepherd's Pie, 62
	Pepperoni & Swiss Knots, 13
	Pizza Squares, 75
	Sausage Pinwheels, 75
Rice	$1 Store Sweet & Sour Chicken/Shrimp, 78
	Fish Fried Rice, 114
	Seafood Jambalaya, 94
Rigatoni	Macaroni and Cheese, 104
Salami	Monte Cristo, 40
	Pineapple & Salami Roll-up, 7
Salmon	Mc$1 Store Eggs Benedict, 117
	Seafood Jambalaya, 94
Salsa	Salsa Burgers, 53
	Southwest Chili Salad, 81
	Empanadas, 15
Sardines	Pescado Garlic Bread, 17
Sausage	$1 Sausage & Peppers Burgers, 50
	Empanadas, 15
	Hot Queso Dip with Tomatoes & Sausage, 19
	Inside Out Burgers, 52
	Mc$1 Store Breakfast Sandwich, 44
	Mc$1 Store Eggs Benedict, 117
	Ms. Branda's Shepherd's Pie, 62
	Salisbury Steak, 101
	Salsa Burgers, 53
	Sausage Pinwheels, 24
Scallops	$1 Store Lobster Rolls, 36
	$1 Store Po' Boy, 48
	Cheese Fondue, 23
	Mini Quiches, 26
	Mock Lobster Pie, 108
	Seafood Jambalaya, 94
	Shrimp and Scallop Quesadilla, 45
Seafood/	
Lobster-Crab Legs	$1 Store Lobster Rolls, 36
	$1 Store Po' Boy, 48
	Mock Lobster Pie, Imitation Lobster, 108

Divalicious Menus with Ingredients Costing $1 or Less

Shrimp	$1 Store Lobster Rolls, 36
	$1 Store Po' Boy, 48
	$1 Store Sweet & Sour Chicken/Shrimp, Popcorn Shrimp, 78
	Cheese Fondue, 23
	Mini Quiches, 26
	Mock Lobster Pie, 1008
	Seafood Jambalaya, 94
	Shrimp and Scallop Quesadilla, 45
Smoked Sausage	Cheese Fondue, 23
	Hot Dogs and Spicy Sauerkraut, 72
	Seafood Jambalaya, 94
Sour Cream	Dill Sauce, 29
Spaghetti Sauce	Meatball Subs, 54
	Pescado Garlic Bread, 17
	Tilapia Rollups, 96
Spinach	$1 Store Ravioli Carbonara, 64
	Baked Eggs Florentine, 69
	Cream of Tomato Soup w/Collard Greens & Blackbeans, 67
	Creamed Spinach, 103
	Baked Eggs Florentine, 69
	Mc$1 Store Eggs Benedict, 117
	Sausage Pinwheels, 24
Stir Fry	
Onions & Peppers	$1 Sausage & Peppers Burgers, 50
	$1 Store Sweet & Sour Chicken/Shrimp, 78
	Cream Chicken Mushroom Corn Chowder, 76
	Fish Fried Rice, 114
	Hot Dogs and Spicy Sauerkraut, 72
	Meatball Subs, 54
	Ms. Branda's Shepherd's Pie, 62
	Salisbury Steak, 101
	Seafood Jambalaya, 94
	Shrimp and Scallop Quesadilla, 45
Stir Fry Vegetables	$1 Store Sweet & Sour Chicken/Shrimp, 78
Strawberries	Ho-Jo Strawberry Shortcake, 162
	Elder Denise's Lemon Berry Parfait, 130
	Strawberry Lemon/Lime Water Ice, 74
Sweet Potatoes	Sweet Potato Biscuits, 154
Tilapia	Fish Fried Rice, 114

Dining With the Dollar Diva

	Mc$1 Store Eggs Benedict, 117
	Mini Quiches, 26
	Mock Lobster Pie, 108
	Seafood Jambalaya, 94
	Tilapia Rollups, 96
Tomatoes	Cream of Tomato Soup w/Collard Greens & Blackbeans, Whole, 67
	Macaroni and Cheese, Stewed, 104
	Seafood Jambalaya, Crushed, Paste, 94
	Southwest Chili Salad, Fresh/Whole, 81
	Pescado Garlic Bread, 17
	Hot Queso Dip with Tomatoes & Sausage, Stewed Tomatoes, 19
	Pescado Garlic Bread, 17
Tortillas	Joe's Chips, 21
	Southwest Chili Salad, 81
Tropical Fruit	$1 Store Foccacia Pineapple Cookie, 141
Tuna	Meatballs & Tuna Bites, 10
Turkey	Monte Cristo Sandwich, 40
Vanilla Pudding	Apple Dumpling w/Warm Custard Sauce , Dry Pudding, 106
	Apple Dumpling w/Warm Custard Sauce, Snack Pack, 106
	Peach Melba, Instant Pudding Mix, 161
	Peach Melba, Vanilla Pudding & Pie Filling, 161
	Vanilla Napoleon Rounds, Instant Pudding, Snack Pack, 126
Waffles	Mc$1 Store Breakfast Sandwich, 44
	Mc$1 Store Eggs Benedict, 117
	Waffle Ice Cream Sandwiches, 73
Walnuts	$1 Store Foccacia Pineapple Cookie, 141
	Cinnamon Apple—Almond Raisin Waffle Panini, 43
	Fellowship Bread, 168
	German Chocolate Brownies, 147
Wasabi Sauce	Chipolte-Wasabi Mayonnaise, 28
Whipped Topping	Ho-Jo Strawberry Shortcake, 162
	Elder Denise's Lemon Berry Parfait, 130
	Peach Melba, 161

Divalicious Menus with Ingredients Costing $1 or Less

Dining With the Dollar Diva

Divalicious Menus with Ingredients Costing $1 or Less

ALSO AVAILABLE FROM THE ELEVATOR GROUP

Cousin Myrtle, a novel, by P. J. McCalla

Heads Deacon, Tails Devil, a novel, by P. J. McCalla

Mr. and Mrs. Grassroots: How Barack Obama, Two Bookstore Owners, and 300 Volunteers Did It, by John Presta

A Student's Guide to Being Happy in Argentina, by Hope Lewis

Land Mines, a novel, by Sheilah Vance

Journaling Through the Land Mines, by Sheilah Vance

Chasing the 400, by Sheilah Vance

AND FROM THE ELEVATOR GROUP FAITH

Rejected for a Purpose: How God Uses Rejection to Help You Find and Fulfill Your Destiny, by O. J. Toks

Creativity for Christians: How to Tell Your Story and Stories of Overcoming from the Members of One Special Church, by Sheilah Vance with Rev. Felicia Howard

For more information about any of the above books, see www.TheElevatorGroup.com or contact us at:

ELEVATOR GROUP
• PUBLISHING •

Helping People Rise Above™

The Elevator Group
45 Darby Road, Suite E-2   Paoli, PA   19301
610-296-4966 (p) 610-644-4436 (f)
info@TheElevatorGroup.com